£12-95

D0865886

Ralph's Far North

Ralph MacGregor

illustrations by Moira Webster

Live adventurously!
Ralph.

Curlew Cottage Books

Published by
Curlew Cottage Books
Curlew Cottage,
Hilliclay Mains,
Weydale, Thurso,
Caithness, KW14 8YN

© text and photographs 2000 Ralph MacGregor

ISBN 0-9538703-0-8

Typeset by
Whittles Publishing Services
Roseleigh House, Latheronwheel,
Caithness, KW5 6DW

Printed by J.W.Arrowsmith Ltd., Bristol

Contents

Contents

Introduction

Live adventurously! That might serve as a sub-title to this personal view of Scotland's far North. Most of the pieces describe travels on foot or by bike, a few venture further afield to foreign lands such as Fair Isle and the North of England. The material is largely based on the 'Out and About with Ralph' column which has appeared fortnightly in the 'Caithness Courier' over many years. If you live south of Inverness you may find it hard to believe that such places as I describe still exist in Britain. Exist they do, come and see for yourself! The Far North is still one of the least known and most beautiful parts of the world.

This is not a conventional guide book on hill-walking or cycling, though you will find that much of the Far North is covered. There are, deliberately, no maps included. If you wish to take any of my routes you'd best purchase a good 1:50000 Ordnance Survey map first and make sure that you can read it. I may write about jogging along cliff-tops or across remote mountains, if you don't feel comfortable doing this yourself, don't. It was safe for me, it may or may not be safe for you, or for children, or for dogs; you must judge for yourself. My advice is that you don't do anything beyond your capabilities, beyond what you feel happy doing – and always be prepared for bad weather. If the mist descends and a blizzard or storm of driving rain suddenly springs up you should be prepared and competent to get safely back to base or you shouldn't be there. You should also have enough experience of weather conditions to have seen it coming! I offer no other advice on equipment, experience, fitness etc, there are countless books, pamphlets and even courses available on these subjects but there is no substitute for common sense.

There are many folk who are more adventurous than me, who climb more mountains, cycle and run further and faster, spend more days and nights out in the hills. There are all those who really know about wild life and botany, about geology and landscape. I'm just an amateur who likes stravaiging in the moors and mountains, particularly in the Far North. If there is anything unusual about me it's that I always go on my own. Company on the hills is fine, but the outing is then a social activity with the surroundings as a backdrop. To properly appreciate the environment, to have time to listen, to see, to think, I have to be alone.

The articles in this book are arranged roughly according to the seasons of the year, remember that Summer is short in the north of Scotland! Dip in at random, read from beginning to end, or simply flip through to look at Moira Webster's delightful drawings. I hope you enjoy the book and that it inspires you to get 'out and about' more, or at any rate to join me in your imagination.

A note on access

Access can be a thorny issue. You may not necessarily have a legal right to take some of the routes described in this book. That being said, until the nineteenth century there was no restriction on access in upland Scotland and there remains a de-facto 'freedom to roam'. Many landowners would however dispute this. You may encounter problems. In my view the important thing is that different interests respect each other's right to use the land.

Deer-shooting (stalking) is a legal activity carried out on most Highland estates and those wishing to cross estate land should give this due consideration, especially during the stag-shooting season between August and late October. However estates must also recognise that ordinary folk have a legitimate right to cross the land and should only impose restrictions when essential, such as in areas and on days when stalking is actually taking place. There can be no excuse at all for restricting access at other times such as during the hind cull (October to February). At that time of year there will be few visitors, especially during the week, and any gamekeeper worth his pay should easily be able to carry out his work without needing to keep people out.

Dire warning notices left up all year, or blanket requests to ask permission are, in my opinion, best ignored. I even saw a permanent notice-board (in Glen Lyon) which insisted that walkers follow a circuit of mountains anti-clockwise! The best solution I have come across, (in the Cairngorms) is a little box at the start of the access track with leaflets showing routes you can take that day without interfering with the stag-stalking.

In Caithness I'm in two minds about privately owned estate land. I sympathise greatly with those estates which are friendly, and are doing their best to conserve the peatlands, flora and fauna. The estate owner could easily have made a quick profit by selling up to the forestry companies a few years ago and will certainly now be running the estate at a loss. In such instances although there is no legal requirement for permission it may be polite to ask, particularly if taking a group of people during the stalking season. On unfriendly estates I will go with no qualms at all, making sure that I'm not seen…

You must settle the matter with your own conscience; usually (but not always) if you seek permission you will get a friendly response. Personally, I will resist strongly any suggestion that permission has to be sought at all times; as a loyal citizen and taxpayer I have the right to cross my own country. Everyone is entitled to some privacy around their house, even in a few acres of land – but not to keep people out of hundreds or thousands of acres.

The onus on visitors to estate and farmland is to respect it, to follow the country code, to behave in a sensible and responsible manner, to make an effort to understand something of the way of life and the problems faced by farmers, crofters and gamekeepers.

There is a small minority of visitors who knows little and cares less about the countryside and those who live and work there. These are the ones whose dogs chase the sheep and the grouse, who throw away litter, break down fences and vandalise bothies. Farmers and gamekeepers can hardly be blamed for being circumspect with visitors if they have encountered people like this. For every 'bad' visitor there are however a hundred who will rescue sheep stuck in bogs or entangled in fences, who will re-unite lost lambs with their mothers, who will report to the farmer injured or sick stock. From a purely practical point of view, open access has much to commend it.

You will still meet the old-fashioned keep-out landowner, the irate keeper, the irascible farmer. Some just don't like people, some believe that because it's their land nobody else should be allowed in, a few have illegal activities to hide such as the setting of pole traps and the poisoning and shooting of eagles and hen-harriers. Often, the better kept and more well run the farm or estate is, the more open about access it is. A bad estate can always find some excuse to keep you out – stag stalking, hind stalking, muirburn, fox denning, lambing, grouse chicks hatching, deer calving etc. etc... a good estate somehow never finds it a problem to get on with these things while still permitting open access.

The recent 'concordat' on access is a big step in the right direction, hopefully 'responsible freedom to roam' on uncultivated land will soon be a legal right, with the right to walk any path or track. The emphasis is at long last moving to a position where people have right of access to all land (with due regard for privacy near dwellings) unless there is an extremely good reason for keeping them out.

Please however don't quote this book if you're challenged; routes taken by me, alone, do nothing to alter the legal rights and wrongs of access.

Ralph

The Caithness skyline

Caithness has, for a supposedly flat county, some very fine mountains. The skyline of Morven and Scaraben is almost a Caithness trademark and what better than a walk along it on a bright Winter day!

Few visit Braemore, fewer still climb the hills, which remain neglected even by those who will drive hundreds of miles to climb more well-known peaks. The Caithness skyline gives a hill walk of the first order but requires an early start and no dawdling in midwinter.

Gales and squally showers had been forecast; I set off prepared for anything and was pleasantly surprised by a fine clear day with only a moderate wind. Never believe the forecast when heading for the hills and always be an optimist!

By the light of a torch I packed up the rucksac and set off in the first glimmerings of dawn along the track from Braemore towards Gobernuisgeach. A roundabout route onto Morven had been deliberately chosen; I like that track out into the heart of the Caithness flow country, particularly on a frosty morning as dawn comes up over the hills.

After a few miles you come abreast of Morven to the south; the temptation to cut straight across is tempered by the knowledge that the Berriedale water is very cold and there is no footbridge before Gobernuisgeach. The track has recently been improved so that a landrover could probably drive to the end of it in only 15 minutes from Braemore, nevertheless the empty house there is still pretty remote.

Six miles of track-walking had been enough and it was nice to give the legs a bit of variety crossing rough country. The ground was surprisingly well frozen, with a sprinkling of snow; in such conditions dubh-lochs and boggy pools give the best going! I was heading for Small Mount, the rarely-visited top west of Morven; to do the skyline proper I really should have included Cnoc an Eireannaich, two miles further west, but there simply was not enough time on a short Winter day.

Patches of old snow, frozen into ice, led to the stony summit ridge. A low sun illuminated the yellow and orange moors casting shadows in the deep valleys cleaving the Knockfin heights; beyond rolled the white slopes of Ben Armine and Klibreck. Cloud clung to Ben Uarie above Glen Loth, banners of mist came and went on Morven. Far to the north, the cliffs of Hoy glowed in the sun. The wind was cold.

The boggy col between Small Mount and Morven was frozen hard and the steep piled boulders on Morven were icy with a light covering of snow and plenty of hoar. This route up Morven, from the 'back' is my favourite, with a good narrow ridge and excellent views.

The view from Morven is one of the best and well worth the effort of the climb. As mist came and went the low sun projected my shadow, complete with triple coloured halo, onto the cloud. No, I'm not suffering from delusions of grandeur; this beautiful sight is fairly common on Winter mountains but very rarely seen elsewhere and is produced in a manner similar to a rainbow.

Not the most expensive restaurant in the world can produce a lunch to compare with a cold snack from a sandwich box eaten in a bitter wind on the top of Morven on such a day. The best things in life are always free, or nearly so.

I warmed up by picking my way carefully down the steep slopes to the col, crossing the partly frozen bogs and climbing back up to the rocky top of Carn Mor. The next top, Smean, is a fantastic place of rock tors, some quite difficult to climb, and eerie on a misty day. It's that crinkly bit you see on the skyline, midway between Morven and Scaraben. Maiden Pap, the sharp peak to the north, is well worth visiting but with the sun already very low there wasn't time.

My next destination was the Toberon Fhionn, where crystal water flows from a spring not half a mile from the top of Smean. It took me years to find this spot so I'll leave its location as an exercise for the reader! The two-and-a-half inch map helps, and the name gives a clue on snowy days. After filling a bottle of water it was time to hurry on, it was only 2.45 but sunset was just 30 minutes away.

As I slowly climbed up the snowfields flanking Scaraben the whole county of Caithness to the north dipped into the sunset shadow. Already, from the west top, the lighthouse of Tarbet Ness could be seen flashing, as well as the lights of the oil-rigs out at sea and the headlights of a car near Lybster. There would just be time to reach the summit proper.

Frozen snow covered many of the stones and, fortunately, gave fast going as dusk deepened. At 3.45 I stood on the summit as the late afternoon light faded, a cold wind blew and the mountains gradually turned to silhouettes. There was little time to linger; I hurried on east, then down the heather slopes as dark grew and Venus appeared shining with amazing brilliance above the ridge I'd just left.

The torch was packed but not needed – just – till back at the car. It would not have been possible to squeeze much more into the short day and I drove out of Braemore as I came in, headlights sweeping across the empty, starlit moors.

A Winter weekend

A shower of snow before leaving work had left the roads white; traffic on the main road would soon render this into a layer of glazed ice. I turned off and pedalled over Shebster Brae to enjoy a quiet ride along the back road to Thurso as dusk fell. Shower clouds were still silhouetted against the sunset sky as I climbed up the long hills from Thurso to Weydale; Jupiter and Venus were bright and there, just visible above the horizon was the faint pinpoint of light that was Mercury. A crescent moon hung between Venus and Jupiter, the rest of the moon faintly visible by 'Earthshine'. You could have drawn a straight line through all four heavenly bodies – a demonstration of the equinoctal plane far more dramatic than any picture in an astronomy book! Just four simple lights in the sky but a magnificent sight.

There was still only a powdering of snow in the morning; we drove out to Loch More in the hope of finding it a bit deeper and indeed there was just about enough snow for a child's skis and sledge on the road. Fishermen were already out after early season salmon, without much success. Only a thin skin of ice covered the loch but the shores were deep in white where ice had repeatedly broken and been blown by the wind to be piled up and refrozen. Tiers of icicles hung down from the overhanging banks and the sandy beaches had a thin snowcover which showed the up the prints of a fox. A patch of clear water reflected the pale blue and white of the moorland scene to the north, to the south streamers of snow moved in over Morven and Scaraben. We set off for home in a whirl of snow that could have been the beginning of a blizzard but was only, alas, a brief flurry.

The last of the snow was disappearing under an onslaught of wind-driven rain as I set out the next morning for a walk. Ruins of old crofts are sad places in such weather. The tumbled walls, where once a warm peat-fire burnt for months on end, now only emphasise the bleakness of the cold rain. There are at least 20 such ruins within a mile of where I live.

Once over Stemster Hill the 'beech avenue' gave some shelter, half a mile of track with a single line of beech trees planted on either side. Wild geese were calling in large numbers from fields west of Loch Stemster, many having wintered to benefit from large acreages of uncut and rotting oats. About six hundred took to the air at once with a roar of wings and a cacophony of honking, a most impressive sight.

The woods around Loch Stemster are rather neglected, though protected by an off-putting (and oft ignored) 'PRIVATE' sign. The loch was covered in ducks, geese and swans – on such occasions I wish I were more of a birdwatcher! The extensive reed-beds must surely hide much of interest in the Summer.

The wind and rain continued to beat down as I made my way back over Stemster Hill, stopping to look at more ruined crofts and a 5000 year-old chambered cairn. Caithness goes back to basics on such a day, just wind, rain, tumbled stones, waves thudding against cliffs, wild birds calling beneath a grey, grey sky. It was almost strange to step back into the warmth and shelter of a modern house, with the elemental strength of the Winter reduced to a faintly heard pattering of rain on the window.

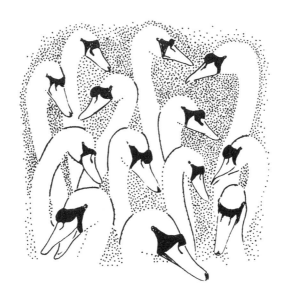

Over the hills and far away

'Over the hills and far away' – an evocative line out of childhood. The hills were far away then and the land beyond only vaguely known. It involved a day's expedition of changing buses for our family to spend a few hours on the low green hills just four miles in a straight line from home.

It is one of the sad consequences of the modern pace of life and of travel that this sense of mystery, of the true scale of distances, has gone. From Thurso you can drive to Dunbeath in less than half an hour and be in Helmsdale in another 20 minutes. Already you are over the hills and far away, probably grumbling that it's taken so long on such a twisty steep road.

I never cross the Ord without thinking of Neil Gunn's description of Katrine's crossing, in his book 'The Silver Darlings'. Dunbeath, viewed from Helmsdale, was a foreign land and it was unheard of for a young lady to manage the journey in a day. To whisk across these hills at 60MPH in a car, or even at 10MPH on a bicycle, has an air of unreality about it.

The new fast roads across the Highlands – the Ullapool road, the A9, the road across the Moine for example – give a similar feeling of unreality. The pace of travel has always been slow in the Highlands with so many difficulties, bogs, rivers, steep passes and wild weather. These smooth new curves of tarmac carved through the landscape seem out of place.

The trains on the Highland line have never been noted for their speed and after a hundred years might be considered part of the landscape. But that sense of unreality is still there at times, particularly on the stretch of the north line from Helmsdale, up Kildonan Strath.

For thousands of years people lived off the land in small communities, the boundary of their world the skylines of the surrounding hills. The railway carves right through some of the sites of homes of only 200 years ago; you are travelling at speed across the hearths where the peat fires never went out. It was

beyond the imagination of the people of the day. The modern equivalent would perhaps be the demolition of Earth to make way for a hyperspace bypass, as in Douglas Adams' 'Hitch-hikers Guide to the Galaxy'!

Modern travel annihilates distance in what is often a very convenient way. Yet we lose a lot when we lose our sense of distance. It is good occasionally to put the pack on one's back, and walk, perhaps 15 or 20 miles a day. Or even to cycle, slowly, without one's head down and an overriding concern to burn up as many miles as possible. You watch the horizons change at the pace man has been familiar with for hundreds of thousands of years, you are keeping time with the world. The hills are a long way off again, the land beyond mysterious, the passes high, the bogs, rivers and storms real obstacles.

'Over the hills and a great way off, the wind has blown my top knot off.'

June at New Year

One car, one bus and one van – all the traffic in a drive of 70 miles along the north coast to the head of Loch Eribol. But then it was very early on the last day of the year!

The light was growing when I left the car and headed for the mountains. Caithness had been mild but here it was positively warm, indeed the day would have been respectable in June. Cloud was well broken and clear of the tops and the wind was light, one almost expected to feel the tickle of the midges.

An area of the lower slopes of Ben Spionnaidh has been ploughed for afforestation – an improvement here where the scale is fairly small, the land of little environmental interest and the climate such that trees should grow. Fish farm expansion has taken place at Polla, formerly a house which stood empty for most of the year. Good to see sensible development in an area where employment is badly needed.

The eastern side of Spionnaidh is basically one large slab of rock tilted at the same angle from the 2500 foot summit to the sea, three miles away. The slab is covered on its lower slopes by a thin layer of poor soil and peat, but is mostly naked higher up with large fields of boulders. A few streams cascade down in waterslides and slabby falls, having failed to carve any depth into the rock.

The most interesting way up is to follow one of the streams to where it peters out in the Lunar zone. One often hears of the mountains of Sutherland described as a moonscape but it is the upper slopes of Spionnaidh and Cranstackie that most fit this description. The landscape is probably one of the rockiest and barest in Britain.

Broken crags fall steeply to the west of the summit of Spionnaidh; far below I could see the empty line of the Durness-Rhiconich road and beyond the barren rolling hills of the Parph, towards Cape Wrath.

It was ridiculously mild for late December, though a gusty wind and the alti-

tude made it comparable to an average afternoon in Thurso. If these warm Winters become more frequent perhaps the ptarmigan will adapt so as not to change colour! As it was, they were most conspicuous in their white plumage against the snow-free, dark grey rock.

I made my way down uncharacteristic grassy slopes to the col below Cranstackie and then up 600 feet of boulder and rock to this higher top with spectacular views of the crags and corries of Foinaven above the desperately boggy Strath Dionard. Southwards the slopes of Cranstackie fall away gently for four miles and again all is boulder and rock with only the occasional patch of mossy grass.

The wind was warm, the sun bright, the tops clear – it seemed like Summer – and yet 70 miles of drive through pitch dark had firmly impressed on my brain that it was Winter. This combined with the peculiar Lunar landscape through which I was making my way gave rise to a feeling of complete unreality such as I can't remember experiencing before on the hills.

So, as in a dream, I picked my way down for an hour, scrambling over the contorted boulders and crags of Conamheall and on to the bealach above Loch Dionard, a loch which lies below the remotest and highest cliffs in the north. I slithered my way down sodden peat to Strath Beag and began to wake up as the sun disappeared below the hills and it seemed a bit more like December again.

Strath Beag is itself a fascinating place. The completely flat valley floor is a raised peat bog through which the river meanders. On the eastern side rise tiers of crags and slopes covered in house-size boulders overgrown with birches. There is at least one spot where an echo will come back to you six or seven times. In hot still weather, rivers of cold air flow down under the boulder-scree slopes to pool in hollows which you can step in and out of as if they were pools of water. Midges are bad, even in May…

I paddled the river – surprisingly not too cold, and picked my way across the bogs to the foot of the steep slopes. A faint path comes and goes, in and out of boulder and fallen tree, slowly leading you down to where the Strath opens out at the empty house of Strabeg.

All that remained was another mile and a half back to the car in the dusk, a cup of tea and a sandwich and then a long drive home as the last light of the old year waned over the waters of Loch Eribol.

Winter commuting

Nice weather we've been having. Either I'm getting old or it's been the windiest Winter spell for a few years – I know, because there have already been half a dozen times when I've abandoned the bike after the five mile ride to Thurso and caught the bus the rest of the way to work. The driver is getting to know me!

It's the odd gale of force nine or ten that shows how outclassed I am on the bike. I'm not sorry to be on the bus, which is being blown about by the squall as the hail hammers onto the windows out of the early morning November blackness. The bus pulls out – and that's a cyclist we're passing! He's standing on the pedals going up Scrabster Brae and still moving into the teeth of the storm. At least one other makes it to work, if late… and for once I don't envy them. I've fought enough gales and hail this Winter already.

Winter is the time of epic rides in force ten gales and sleet. There is the exhilarating experience of hitting a patch of rutted ice in the dark at 20 miles an hour, the gentle caress of seventy-mile-an-hour hail, the restful dark of a quiet country road when your lights have failed, the invigorating exercise of a two hour ride home when a deep low is sitting over South Cromarty and the south-easterly force nine is driving rain into your face. As a Winter cyclist you've arrived when you make it into work on a particularly ferocious morning to find that all the cars and buses are late and that not one of a thousand other workers has come in by bike.

A couple of times I've set out in a stiff breeze and continued through Thurso in a near gale to be met with a storm a couple of miles on and by standing on the pedals and using most of my strength have just managed to keep going round the DOWNHILL bends at the top of Forss straight. Battling in bottom gear along the last two miles, head down at six miles an hour with one eye shut to keep out the sleet, you can be sure that someone will pedal past, seemingly effortlessly, with some comment to the effect that its a fine day … good Tour De France tactics I suppose.

You get so used to the wind and weather that anything less than force seven when its not actually sleeting or hailing is indeed a fine day and a nice, warm, downpour of gently blowing rain is a most welcome change. There have been few rides in the last month without at least one statutory snow or hail shower and many slow, steady pushes into a force eight or more.

A good gale from behind, on the back road home, is something else though, especially if its snowing or hailing. I pedal along at 30–35 miles an hour with the flakes or pellets drifting gently around while at the same time ricocheting and sweeping down the road in white ribbons. A few lightning flashes and rumbles of thunder from a particularly vicious shower add to the spice of life and its just as I'm pushing up the hill as hard as possible to get home without being struck by lightning that the bottom bracket starts emitting screeching, wailing noises and threatens to seize up solid…

Hard pedalling of up to 150 miles a week through salt, grit, slush and water isn't good for the bike. It was the second bottom bracket this Winter to fail, two cables have broken and the derailleur is worn out. The new gears I put on last October are already worn, a pair of pedals and a chain have been thrown away and a front chainwheel has needed replacing. The wheels and frame are covered in rust and the headset bearings are loose with frequent oiling producing a dirty brown ooze. Would any bike manufacturer care for me to road-test his product through a Caithness winter or two?

December and early January are DARK. It's an experience to take the Broubster road in the early morning in rare calm weather, leaving home in pitch dark, arriving at work in pitch dark, after 20 miles of cycling on dark, empty roads. Then it's pitch dark again for leaving site in the afternoon…

It can be spectacular, with a full moon as bright as day, shooting stars every minute or two and sudden flashes from lightning in shower clouds up to 100 miles away. You become familiar with the changing phase of the moon, the motion of the planets, the rising and setting of different constellations. On a clear dark night you can look up from the road ahead and see the Andromeda galaxy, two million light-years away.

There's a certain camaraderie amongst the winter cyclists. Two together are more likely to be seen by sleepy drivers with misted windscreens on a wet night. Also some feel a strange need for company when pushing into a gale of sleet with sodden icy feet in the blackness on an empty road – see a red rear light in the distance ahead and they'll go flat out to catch up. Even the dedicated racers will slow up for a natter instead of tearing past, as in the Summer, to be home in time for the evening's time trial.

Until it is completely dark you don't need lights to see, only to be seen. On empty country roads it is tempting to save the batteries and switch on the front light only when a car comes. One evening in November I was speeding down to Loch Calder from Brawlbin, enjoying the sight and sound of a skein of geese flying overhead in the twilight. Suddenly the barrel of a shotgun appeared from a ditch, raking me as it was swung up towards the birds. I don't know which of us two lawbreakers got the bigger fright, but he didn't get his goose and I never took that road again in the dusk without a front light!

There was a dark morning when a bus driver nearly forced one of Scotland's faster riders into the ditch on Scrabster Brae. This man could put on quite a sprint when goaded and promptly overtook the bus, hammering on the driver's window and shouting curses as he passed. (He too got a shock once when one of the ordinary cyclists hurtled past him at about 35MPH shortly after leaving site, having grabbed the back of a motor-bike and let go just at the right moment…)

Another cyclist would sometimes take a shortcut across a field, thereby cutting out about a mile of road – until the night he discovered, too late, that the field had been spread with slurry…

On one occasion, two cyclists battling into the teeth of a south-easterly on the Lythmore road passed an American who was trying to cycle home from the base and had stopped in the quarry to wait for the wind to go down. That gale lasted two weeks; perhaps he's still there.

Aye well, its never too bad and now there's some daylight for riding home. Spring will come eventually, and at least I should be fit and able to enjoy the cycling … provided I'm not completely exhausted and can afford a new bike!

History

'Write all you know about the Old Stone Age'. I duly regurgitated my notes, earned seven out of ten – and that is all I can remember of school history. It was scarcely relevant to a child of the fifties when the emphasis was on the future, on all things new, and the past was best forgotten.

In Caithness the past is, however, too much part of the present to be ignored. In this hard northern land, intensive farming and industry have not obliterated the evidence of thousands of years of man's activities, as they have further south.

History is a presence felt, shouting at you, not easily ignored unless you never leave the towns. Almost every day I cycle below the cairns on Cnoc an Freiceadain. Occasionally I stop and climb up to them, communal burial chambers 5000 years old with the remains of walls enclosing courtyards where, perhaps, ceremonies were held. Ten minutes later I'm into the 21st century at Dounreay, a contrast hard to grasp. Yet people were the same then as now.

Often I take the Broubster road home. You cannot miss the grassy piles of stones and ridged fields where people lived until the early nineteenth century before being cleared out to make way for the sheep. Some of them were resettled in a square of terraced houses further down the glen, the road passes right through the middle of this village, now ruinous.

Then there was the old school, closed in the fifties. Dounreay came too late to save Broubster and the last inhabitant left her home in the old schoolhouse a few years ago. The school has now been completely demolished, only the drystone walls which bounded the playground remain. Even the church has finally been stripped of pews and pulpit and turned into a barn. The manse remains, a solid house as big as the church, but empty as it has been for 40 or more years.

Out on the moors, the last few hundred years can be read like a book. In a green oasis are lines of parallel, low ridges which were the lazy-beds where muck, seaweed, old turf from roofs or anything else fertile was heaped up so that oats

could be grown. Overgrown squares of stones mark the broken-down low walls of the pre-clearance houses. Sometimes you can see the holes where the roof crucks, long roots of ancient pine trees rescued from the peat, were fitted. Sometimes also there is the ruin of a circular kiln, perhaps built on to the end of a long house, where the oats, harvested green were dried.

A more recent ruin with a fine wall of dressed stone and a gable-end is where the shepherd lived until the turn of the century, tending the sheep which replaced the people. Then, over the hill, is the turretted architecture of a big lodge-house built when deer-stalking for the wealthy replaced sheep farming. Now the lodge itself is empty, slowly decaying and surrounded by miles of struggling pine and spruce – the deer are, in turn, being replaced by tree farming.

Two or three thousand years after the chambered cairns came the brochs, the remains of which can be found everywhere in the county. In these tall, circular, fortified stone towers the Iron-Age people lived as in multistorey blocks of flats. Recent by comparison are the Viking settlements such as you can see at Reay and Freswick. The Viking rubbish tips or middens now take the form of a dark stratum in the sand dunes where sea has eroded. You can pull out limpet shells, bits of bone and charcoal – the remains of meals of 700 years ago.

It was not a peaceful time and further centuries of warfare are marked by the castles which are crumbling into ruin every few miles along our coasts. Some occupy spectacular and almost impregnable positions on narrow ridges between two deep geos, sometimes old dungeons still remain...

Almost yesterday the herring fishings came, and went, leaving their mark on the east coast all the way from Freswick to Berriedale. Go down any accessible (or even pretty inaccessible) bay or cove and you will find old piers, tall roofless buildings, rusting winches, rings set in the rock and eroding steps.

Yet thousands of years of man's activities have really had very little impact on Caithness. It is the natural world that still dominates – the storms, the sky, the light, the cliffs, the birds, the vast moors. Its a comforting thought that, whatever mess man makes of the world, Caithness will look much the same in another 5000 years.

From dawn to dusk on Ben Loyal

Ben Hiel has the distinction of being a peak that is almost invariably climbed by mistake. I've done it myself when setting off for Ben Loyal from Loch Loyal. If you don't look at the map carefully, you assume the steep slopes rising to the south-west lead straight onto the main ridge of Loyal. You get a nasty surprise when you reach the summit of Ben Hiel and find you then have to descend nearly 1000 feet to get onto the slopes of Ben Loyal proper.

Ben Loyal deserves more than just a quick nip up and down by the shortest route. To do the mountain justice on a short day at the turn of the year needed an early start, so it was just after eight when I left the car above Loch Loyal.

There is a little path which contours round Ben Hiel, but not easy to find in the dark. By taking the obvious route I eventually came across it; there is only one best way across rough country. Above the col, steep slopes of heather turning to grass led up towards the main ridge. A red glow in the east caught my eye; the sun was just rising below a thin sheet of cloud which covered these western hills.

Has anyone ever visited all the tops of Ben Loyal on a single walk? All are well worth exploring, leisurely and carefully, but I always end up missing out one or two! Ben Hiel had already been omitted but I made sure of going out to the northernmost top which gives a dramatic view down to the Kyle of Tongue. The rocks were icy and care was needed, though the main ridge only bore the odd patch of frozen snow. The day was indeed remarkable for this normally stormy time of year; although well below freezing there was only the lightest of southerly breezes, with clear views all round.

In spite of its dramatic aspect when seen from lower down, the main ridge of Ben Loyal is a smooth grassy plateau. Rocky tors mark the tops of the craggy eminences seen from below. There is a nice patch of smooth grass at the very summit which once gave me an excellent site on which to pitch a tent and see the sunset and dawn. There is even a nearby spring! Crags fall vertically to the east and there is no easy way off the summit to the south; you must first go back the way you came until off the summit rocks.

The highest vertical cliffs on the mountain fall away from the last-top-but-one to the narrow Loch Fhionnaich, and this summit is a fine eyrie indeed. There is no safe northwards descent other than to go back east, down easy slopes to the loch then to climb up another 500 feet to cross the last main peak which, although prominent in all photos of Ben Loyal, is very rarely visited.

Once again, steep crags bar a direct descent and it is safest to take the gentler slopes to the south-west. I was in any case heading for Loch an Dherue which is an obligatory visit in any circuit of Ben Loyal. The steep crags and woods marking its eastern shore are one of the more delightful and unusual places in the North and well worth a detour of many miles! Anyone trying to descend directly to the loch will arrive there much sooner than planned; it is necessary to go well south before striking west, coming down to Dherue bothy.

The bothy is now, sadly, in a bad way and the estate would obviously rather let it fall down than have it renovated by volunteers. A new estate road passes the very door, though years ago it had a much more remote aspect. Once I was overnighting in a very dry spell when a huge moorland fire was approaching from the south. I had to spend a lot of time and sweaty effort beating out flames which were encroaching dangerously.

The path through the birches and boulders along the eastern shore of the loch is magic. There are many fine echo spots from the crags above, but it is a shame to make a noise and disturb the peace. Many a day could be spent exploring the complex tangle of boulder, crag and tree.

There was now a slight thaw in progress, and it was completely calm. I'd just left the northern end of the loch when a roar, a bit like a low-flying jet, made me turn round to see several cubic metres of boulders bouncing down the hillside from a small landslip. I saw a tree-trunk flying into the air before the whole lot came to a stop only yards from where I'd just been walking. What can you do? I shrugged my shoulders and carried on.

I always like this walk along the western slopes of Ben Loyal, with the steep birch woods rising up towards the crags. It was getting late though and I had to hurry, climbing up above the old Cunside farm in the dusk and picking my way across the peat workings below Ben Hiel as darkness fell. The car was still there, and after a day in the empty Sutherland Hills I drove home on deserted roads listening to news of cities and motorways jammed with traffic coming home from the January sales.

January days

I've not managed to get far in the last few weeks. It's been pretty wild and stormy, particularly at weekends, but that's no excuse. Maybe I'm just falling prey to middle if not old age!

A week ago my plans were for an expedition over Ben Armine by bike, from Kinbrace to Lairg with the train each way. Perhaps January was a silly month to contemplate such a thing. Anyway, with a forecast for a day of gales and severe blizzards on the hills it just wasn't on. A less adventurous outing was called for.

Come the morning and just about the worst conditions possible. The overnight snow had turned to deep wet slush, too soggy for skiing. Driving the car anywhere other than Thurso would be plain stupid. Rain and sleet continued to lash down, driven by the gale. Cycling, even if possible, would be purgatory. Walking, dressed to the hilt against the conditions would be a slow plod through the wet snow.

The only thing to do, other than going back to bed, was to put on a light cagoule, overtrousers, and an old pair of running shoes and set off for a few miles' jog over the hill. Once you've got going you keep warm, move fast, and can enjoy the wild conditions.

I'm usually jogging over Olrig Hill at least once a week, often in the pitch dark in Winter, so splashing through the slush and mud in the half-light and a gale of sleet was nothing out of the ordinary. The snow had been drifting up near the masts, but was now slowly thawing; I splashed and slithered on down the road through the Olrig woods, enjoying the shelter of the trees. Further on, I turned off into the woods – and there were the January snowdrops, tightly in bud but bravely showing above the snow. Something thought it was Spring! (AND I heard the first lark singing on Keiss links, just a week later)

Back home the snowplough had been through but the rain and sleet had set in for the rest of the day. Not even the garden could be dug, saturated and hidden under the wet snow! So, another activity where one can laugh at the weather – off to the Thurso pool for a swim.

There are still one or two people in Caithness who swim every day… in the sea! I have seen bare footprints through the snow on Keiss beach. I like outdoor 'wild' swimming myself but the weather has to be warm. One of my favourite places is the pair of deep rock pools at Oigins geo, just along from Dounreay. On a summer lunchtime I can jog there, have a ten minute swim and get back to the office all in half-an hour. When the tide is high and waves are breaking into the pool – who needs jacuzzis! Given our Summers, though, there are some years when I never quite seem to manage even one outdoor dip. On a raw, sleety day a heated indoor pool is definitely the place to be.

Anyone with a bit more get-up-and-go would have headed for the high hills the next day, the snow was hard frozen, the wind dropped and the sun appeared. At least Olrig hill still had enough snow to enjoy gentle cross-country skiing around the fields and on the slopes down from the mast. The next day would have given rare perfect conditions for cross-country skiing over the moors but work called.

By lunchtime the sky was clear and blue, the wind light, the hills above 200 feet still white. There was just about time to cycle out of site, tear up the tracks through the old Boston camp, leave the bike and race up onto the top of Cnoc an Freiceadain. Unblemished, frozen snow. Blue sea with the white rolling hills of Hoy beyond and the Ola, a speck in the distance, bound for Stromness. White mountains marching along the western horizon – Ben Hee, Loyal, Hope, Foinaven, Spionnaidh, Cranstackie – it wouldn't last, already the south wind was picking up. Run back to the bike, hurtle back to site – what a rush, but worth the effort.

Usually the wind settles in the west, or the south-east around now – but not this year! Every day it's been different, usually at least force six, from the north, the east, the south, the west, often with squalls of rain, sleet or hail and somehow managing to give a headwind on the bike both in the evening and on the following morning. But it's getting light now, and what a difference that makes! I may not be getting far, but at least I can see something of the county every day from the bike, be it the waterfalls blowing back over the cliffs near Brims or a kestrel hovering over Broubster.

The snow's melting off the hills and the days are lengthening; realistically we all know there are probably months of Winter still to come but maybe there will be a day for that trip across Ben Armine yet!

Through dark and snow

I'd been cycling for two and a half hours. It was a quarter past seven in the morning on the first of February. It was snowing.

My destination was a small village on the edge of the Yorkshire Dales, near Kirkby Stephen. By leaving Thurso on the late afternoon train I could catch the London train from Inverness and be in Preston at a quarter to five the next morning. That left 65 miles to cycle.

The forecast had been good, promising a rising south wind to blow me northwards, and the moon would be nearly full. Envisaging a moonlit cycle along country lanes and a frosty dawn in the hills, I chose a route through the high moors of the Forest of Bowland and then across the Dales.

Any lingering doubts about cycling north (rather than waiting for another train to take me nearer my destination) vanished as I unloaded the bike from the guards' van. Preston is not my favourite station and at 4.45AM on a freezing first of February was at its bleakest. A few travellers were pacing up and down the waiting room like lost souls in Hell as I cycled thankfully down the platform and up the ramp out of the station.

My only map was an old quarter-inch sheet which gave little help in finding my way out of the town. Cycling down a wide, deserted street I saw two policeman and stopped to ask the way out to Longridge. 'Just carry straight on, out to Ribbleton – and by the way you're cycling the wrong way down a one-way street!'

I cycled for miles past factories, garages and houses along deserted roads. The moon had gone and the wind was easterly, but it was dry and not too cold. Eight miles on, at Longridge, the real fun started.

Much of rural England is a maze of little roads and you need a good map to find your way. The scale of my map was a bit small; at every turn I had to stop and peer at it in the light of the bike's front lamp. Now, out in the country, it was really black; only the farms were lit up, with the sound of milking machines and the smell of cows as I passed.

A few motes were appearing in the beam of my light – surely not flies? They got a bit more frequent – must be rain – then, as they thickened up I realised to my horror that it was snowing. Perhaps just a local flurry over the hills – but I was now committed to my route over steep roads to Slaidburn and then across a 1400-foot pass to Bentham. As I hurtled down one hill, eyes screwed up to keep the snow out, the surprised voice of a farmer bid me good morning from the 6.30AM darkness; I responded with an equally surprised 'aye' and pedalled on up the next hill…

At Slaidburn, in the first glimmers of dawn, I stopped and pondered. The town of Settle, and a late morning train north to Kirkby Stephen was only ten miles away. North lay my planned route over the pass, 12 miles through wet cold snow to Bentham and another 35 to go after that. The light came on in a cottage across the road and a lady clad in dressing gown opened the door to bring in the milk. An empty school bus roared past up the hill; morning village life was just starting. The snow continued drifting gently down and would it ever get light?

The decision was made. Having come this far I'd be adventurous and push on. I gulped a couple of sandwiches, swigged some orange juice, tied my feet up in polythene bags to keep them dry and set off for the pass.

The road had been well salted and, in spite of the falling snow, remained clear. First came a series of steep ups and downs, with Stocks Reservoir somewhere below in the now growing half-light. A steep descent led to a moorland valley and then a long climb up to the crest of the pass. A few sheep peered at me through the falling snow, icicles hung down banks beside the road. The wind was rising, but fortunately from behind. At last the summit and a sign telling me I was now in the jurisdiction of the City of Lancaster! The Lancastrians had not, however, salted the road as well as the Yorkshiremen and the road this side was covered in snow. Faster than was safe I raced down the hills through slippery slush, eyes screwed up against the snow, hands tight on the brakes.

Out of the moors, into the farmland – then suddenly houses appeared and I slithered to a halt at a busy road junction in the middle of the bustling village of High Bentham. The town clock was just striking nine and it was still snowing.

Crowds of Friday morning shoppers were out and the road was jammed with cars and lorries where roadworks were in full swing. Youngsters were going to school. Somewhat dazed after hours of empty roads I wheeled the bike to a sheltered spot, wiped away the plastered snow from my clothes and had another think. A cuppa would be nice but I'd better push on before the roads got too bad.

A swig of cold juice would have to do, and another sandwich, then off across country, to Burton in Lonsdale and Kirkby Lonsdale. No, I wasn't crossing another pass to Dent as originally planned!

Now, near sea level, the snow was wet and I soon had to stop to don waterproofs. Oh for a cup of hot tea – and wonder of wonders, there was a mobile van by the Devils Bridge at Kirkby Lonsdale. A great mug of steaming tea with two spoons of sugar – heaven! it gave me strength for the next ten miles to Sedbergh.

From this little market town with its cobbled main street a lovely quiet road climbs up the Rawthey valley below the Howgill Fells and onto the moors of Ash Fell before descending to Kirkby Stephen. I'd taken the 14-mile route many times by car or bus, but never cycled it and soon found that the scenery paled in the face of a six-mile long climb of 1000 feet into the wind. A fine drizzle of snow pellets blowing into my eyes ensured that I saw little but the road as I ground on up the hills, milestone slowly passing milestone.

Just past the top of the hill, the road joins a trunk road linking the A66 to the M6, thronged with lorries and traffic. The snow had turned heavier again and with eyes nearly shut against it, going as fast as I could risk, the steep hill down to Kirkby Stephen was not pleasant. The most dangerous part of the journey was the main street of the town in bad visibility with cars and lorries and shoppers playing dodgems and nobody seeing a near-invisible bike.

Twenty hours earlier I'd left Thurso. I'd been cycling for seven and a half hours. It was now midday. It was still snowing.

A night in Glen Feshie

February is my favourite Winter month. The dark of December and January has gone, yet the weather is still often spectacular. If it rains, it rains inches. If it snows, blizzards rage for days in the mountains. If it's sunny, it's brilliant and clear. If the wind blows, it will be a gale, for day after day.

February would be my first choice of any month, Summer or Winter, for travelling around Britain. There may be the odd delay due to snow or floods, but already there are hints of Spring. Nobody goes away in February and so everywhere is quiet, places are themselves, the only people about are locals.

This month, a work trip took me to Manchester and rather than come straight back, I took a few days off to visit relatives further north and then wander back by train.

It had been wet, rather than snowy in the far north of England. The high fells would sometimes have a few inches of snow lying before this was washed off by the next belt of rain, nearly everything was in a state of saturation. The train out of Carlisle hurtled through one downpour after another, watched by sodden sheep in fields half-covered by pools of water.

The character of the light always seems to change when crossing the border and towards Glasgow the air became clearer and colder. White cumulonimbus clouds towered between patches of blue sky, with long views to snow covered hills partly hidden in veils of sleet and hail.

I like to travel with a small rucksac, rather than a hold-all; this gives much more flexibility. In with my work papers were a tightly-rolled light-weight down sleeping bag, a light cagoule and overtrousers, a pair of trainers and a torch. All the equipment needed for a night in the hills, provided I didn't plan to go too high and risk becoming another statistic. My plan was to leave the afternoon train at Kingussie, walk ten miles out to a bothy in Glen Feshie and then return for the early morning train to Inverness and on to Caithness.

Snow was going to be a problem. Already at Blair Atholl there was a sprinkling, and as the train climbed Drumochter the depth rapidly increased to several inches, blowing, with more coming down. A long walk in the dark through deep snow did not appeal but then there mightn't be another chance... That, and the fact that the train was packed with people standing, decided me. At five on a clear, cold late afternoon I alighted at Kingussie and set off down the road.

The hills were very white but there was only an inch or so lying in the strath and the wind had dropped. My route was simple, along the road for three miles then via paths and tracks across to Glen Feshie. Simple on an ordinary day would however be a bit less so on a dark snowy night...

The walk down the road was most enjoyable after the hours on trains, already there was a hard frost and the evening light was fading on the hills. From Tromie Bridge I found the track without bother, the snow now a bit deeper.

It was a pity that the train had been half an hour late into Kingussie... there was one awkward bit of route finding which I'd hoped to still have daylight for. My map was old and didn't mark any of the new forests. Footbridges come and go with the floods. The difficulties could have been avoided by a detour of two miles but this didn't appeal. So it was nearly dark when I reached the tricky bit.

A footbridge still stood, more or less, half on its side and most of the wood gone. It was still just possible to cross. Ahead was a ruin, which the path should pass. Trying to make the most of the last glimmer of daylight I pushed on hard, through heather covered in snow. Things didn't seem quite right. There was a big stream, almost a river which shouldn't be there. Studying the map by torch made me gradually realise that I'd passed the wrong ruin. The compass confirmed that my bearing was 90 degrees out.

No need to panic. The compass told me to head just right of Mars, now brilliant yellow in the constellation of Leo. Splash through the stream (not particularly warm...). Make for the edge of the forest, nevermind how rough and wet the going. Follow the forest edge till I must meet the track where it enters the woods. Floundering through snow-covered heather in the pitch dark was what I'd hoped to avoid!

By 7PM I was back on course, crunching through six inches of snow on the forest track down to the Feshie. This joined the private road to Glen Feshie Lodge which, to my delight, had been cleared of snow by a tractor. Just a three mile walk down the glen now, hardly needing the torch, the stars a brilliance you rarely see even in Caithness with the claws of Cancer as bright as you'd normally expect to see the Plough. To the left the river, with dim snowy slopes beyond rising to the plateau. Deer scattered and regrouped. Silence except for my frozen trainers crunching on the ice.

The lights of the Keeper's house appeared ahead, then a footbridge and a well-trodden path through scattered Scots Pines to the bothy, empty and quiet beneath the stars. 8.15PM. Lots of wood and kindling there for a much antici-pated fire – but no matches. And I'd forgotten to bring any. So by the dim light of my torch I munched cold sandwiches, drank cold water and retreated quickly into a warm sleeping bag!

It wasn't yet six when I set off back for Kingussie, giving myself plenty of time to catch the 9.30 train. A magnificent morning, the mountains bright in the light of a half-moon. As I crunched back down the road, white with a thin covering of fresh snow, the dawn light gradually grew over the Feshie hills.

The wind was rising. I could see clouds of snow blowing off the plateau, it looked pretty wild up there. Gusts of wind shook showers of snow off the forest trees. The bottle of water I'd filled for the journey was already freezing, making rattling rather than sloshing sounds as I walked.

Back at civilisation, Tromie Bridge, the school bus was just picking up chil-dren as the first real snow-shower began. I'd been lucky, the weather deterio-rated over the next hour to wind-driven large flakes of wet snow. Back in Glen Feshie conditions would be getting slow and difficult.

There was just time to buy some food in Kingussie and get back to the station for the train… to discover it was stuck at Dalwhinnie with frozen points and signals. Indeed a train-load of people spent an anxious 45 minutes there, staring out at a worsening blizzard until the points were cleared. But nice to sit back on the warm train when it eventually arrived, less can be said for the lukewarm cup of tea which cost nearly a pound! I decided to stick with my iced water for the rest of the journey.

February is a great month to travel by train. What better than to sit back in comfort watching the gale-driven hail lashing across bleak moorland outside the window (except perhaps to have a HOT cup of tea to go with it!)

Winter sports

Caithness might seem an unlikely Winter sports resort. Gales of sleety rain are hardly the weather for displaying the latest ski-fashions! The clay farmland turns into a sea of mud in the average December whilst the peat moors are at their bleakest, saturated with water and almost devoid of life.

All is transformed, however, after a few days of hard frost. Mud and peat freeze fast, and suddenly you can stride out across what before was a clarty slog in wellies. A bright day then gives most exhilarating conditions for a long walk, whether over farmland or the moors. Inland there may be plenty of snow, with old drifts piled up along the walls and slabs. One of the most characteristic sights of Caithness in February or March is of the yellow fields streaked with those long lines of white, awaiting, as they say, more snow to take them away.

Just one inch of snow on frozen ground is enough for messing around on skis, nothing serious, but great fun for a youngster in learning to slide down gentle slopes. There is often enough for practising a bit of cross-country along the drifts by the walls, even when the rest has melted.

Has skating gone out of vogue these days? Not, I mean, the Torvill and Dean stuff, but the simple pleasure of skating round a frozen loch or pool on a fine day. Certainly I've never seen anyone else on skates, which is a pity as the county must be one of the best places in Britain for outdoor skating. After a wet spell many fields have shallow ponds which freeze quickly and can provide excellent ice with complete safety.

My skating technique is non-existent, but by dint of flailing arms and legs I can just about keep my balance on a pair of ex jumble-sale ice-skates and go roughly in the right direction, which is all that's needed for enjoyment

Early one Sunday morning I set of gingerly by car on roads where skates might well have been better than wheels. Beyond Westerdale the road was snow-covered and at Loch More all was white, calm and very cold. Dawn was still half an hour off but with snow and a clear sky it was light, the mountain outline sharp on the horizon.

Keeping well clear of the outflow I chipped a hole in the ice – four inches thick, ample for safety. One should not, I suppose, recommend skating on frozen lochs; the danger is obvious. If you have any doubts about whether the ice is thick enough, or don't know your loch, keep away. Beware of where rivers enter and leave and of narrows, and if the ice is very smooth take care you're not trapped on it, unable to climb back up a gentle slope to the shore!

Though easily accessible, Loch More has a very remote feel to it in wintry conditions, particularly towards the far end. To skate along the unblemished white surface, in the clear frosty air of a Caithness dawn with Ben Alisky and Morven glowing pink in the rising sun, was a rare experience.

About an inch of powdery snow covered the ice but below this the surface was mostly smooth and the skates sliced through the powder as if it wasn't there. Foxes had crossed the loch in a couple of places but there were no other animal tracks on the ice. Here and there a harmless crack snaked outwards, caused by subsiding or moving ice. In one section wind had piled the ice up into ridges and I had to take the skates off and change into the trainers I'd carried with me. Most of the loch however gave a smooth, steady slide, whisking through the snow, watching the banks coast past. It took about an hour to skate the four miles round the loch, by the end of which time my ankles had had quite enough!

Not being a mountaineer and never having carried ice-axe or crampons, the Caithness hills in Winter are about my standard. Morven in snow feels feels like a much higher peak, though the frequent cackle of the grouse, or the sight of a grey Alpine hare running off over the steep slopes, showed that the icy slopes rising into the January mists were not some high Munro. Perhaps an ice-axe would have been handy; it was slow and hard work kicking steps in frozen snow where the slopes were steepest. Although a slip would only have meant a slide of a few yards, the ascent of the North Gully gave just a taste of the real thing. On the summit, a howling wind across ice made walking difficult – yes, crampons might have helped for a short distance!

An occasional gap in the clouds showed the view west across miles of white and brown but never cleared enough for a photo. The slightly gentler eastern slopes gave an easier descent, apart from slipping into the odd waist-deep hole hidden in snow. Frozen conditions are excellent for crossing the normally boggy plateau of Smean and Carn Mor, to the east of Morven. Even though a thaw was on the way the ground was still hard and gave rapid progress across the various tops. Smean is one of my favourites with its maze of rock tors on the summit, though I've never been there on anything other than a day when it's far too cold and windy to linger.

Detouring first to the secret Toberon Fhionn (to collect a flask of the true water of life!) I headed for Maiden Pap, the last peak of the day. For those who find Morven too much of a climb this little rocky peak, though steep, is a much shorter walk and gives almost as good a view. On top was a walker, out for the afternoon – it was the first time either of us had ever met anyone else there (and how many were on the Aviemore ski slopes?).

Caithness is certainly not the place for convivial Winter sports and apres-ski! But to enjoy an unspoiled and beautiful landscape, far from the madding crowd, at the most spectacular time of year, it is unbeatable.

Stone Lud and Achtoty

After many years in the North, I still find new places to visit and explore, even within a few miles of home – and there are always surprises. It was turning towards dusk on a cold grey Sunday afternoon in early February. There weren't many jobs to do in the garden and the rest of the family had retreated indoors, yet it seemed a pity to waste the remaining hour or so of daylight. A bike ride seemed a good idea, but where?

I'd been reading Calder's 'History of Caithness' and remembered a reference to a tall standing stone – 'Stone Lud' – near Brabsterdorran. It was one of those places which I'd meant to visit sometime but never quite got round to it. A glance at the map showed that it was only about four miles ride and another half mile's walk from home; there was just enough time before dark.

Twenty minutes later I was bumping on the bike down a muddy track through a small forestry plantation near Sibster, leaving behind a flock of very disappointed sheep who had mistaken me for the farmer bearing food. The track came to an end in a wide expanse of grass-cum-moor, sloping up towards the skyline where, what looked from this distance like a small tree, could be seen overtopping a stone wall.

Here too, was evidence of an old road, sunk below ground level with raised mounds on either side. It led, for a few hundred yards, towards that skyline. Apart from a few fences the landscape must have looked very similar when that stone was erected, 1000 years ago in memory of a Viking chieftain, if Calder is to believed.(I suspect in fact that Calder is wrong and that the stone has been there for several thousand years) There was a high, bleak feel to the place, accentuated by the appearance of two or three ruined and deserted crofts near the stone. Tall indeed, ten feet high and pointing up into the darkling grey February sky which looked more than ever like dissolving into sleet. It felt a long way from home and the 1990s.

Another day and another place I'd looked at for many years but never really explored. Heavy rain and low cloud suggested a coastal walk; I'd have a really good look at that interesting stretch of coast between Invernaver and Skerray. The huge expanse of the Torrisdale Sands and the dunes stretching halfway up the cliffs are well seen from the Bettyhill hotel and must must be one of the most unusual views in Britain.

From Invernaver I set off in steady rain, crossing the hummocks where old settlements lie buried, walking across the soft sands and low dunes to where the brown Naver was rushing out into the open sea. The little Bettyhill harbour is just across from here and at low tide and low water it may be possible to wade the gap.

These sandflats when seen from Bettyhill usually seem to be swept by blowing sand; this time the light winds and steady rain gave good conditions in which to follow the coast on round to the big inlet of the Borgie. Here a detour to the footbridge half a mile upstream was needed, returning on the other side along the road past the Torrisdale Crofts to the little cemetery at Torrisdale. This area is rightly popular with tourists in the Summer but a walker on a wet February day was unheard of – so much so that a passing car stopped and the driver wound his window down to comment on the weather – and people were peering out of the windows of the crofts as I walked past.

The stretch of coast along the 'back' of Achtoty was my next objective, a couple of miles that I had somehow never managed to walk. Strange how every bit of the north coast is different; this too had its own character, very different from that just a few miles back. The cliffs were mostly low and broken with some sudden holes opening down to the sea, waterslides ran down into black, rocky coves. In Summer the grassy slopes give good displays of the rare Scottish Primrose and Globe Buttercup. Just across the narrow channel of Kyle Beg is Neave Island, with an enticing looking sandy beach; another place I've yet to visit. Many hundreds of years ago there was a monastic settlement on the island and it is said that people on the mainland would gather to listen to the sermon shouted across the Kyle. Modern ministers and churchgoers have a cushy life…

I rounded the point to the harbour at Skerray, a fine sandy bay, and then climbed up over the next headland as the wind suddenly increased, blowing warm drizzle across in sheets. Dimly, I could see the fresh snow on Ben Hutig. Another sandy bay, Lamigo, opened out below with a swollen burn pouring down a rocky valley; I scrambled down, crossed the beach and set off round the next point. The rain was now dying out but on a coast as full of interest as this you hardly notice what the weather is doing. The cliffs led me round to the third and last little sandy bay, Port an t-Strathain, another delectable spot and requiring a walk to reach it from the nearest road.

Here I turned back, cutting across the hills with the wind behind, over to Skerray then up onto the moor behind Achtoty to come down the burn at Torrisdale. Another couple of miles up over the hill and down the steep slopes to Invernaver and I was back at the car – and another little bit of the Far North explored.

The Hell of the North

From Lands End to John O' Groats has been cycled in under 48 hours. 860 miles non-stop! To me, this is just inconceivable. Just as impossible is the way that racing cyclists can easily manage 100 miles in around four hours; last Saturday it took me nearly ten to cover a similar distance.

My tour was, though, meant to be enjoyed. It was the obvious round trip, down to Dunbeath, over the Ord, up Kildonan and down Halladale, returning home by Shebster and Broubster. For early February, the weather was marvellous, the sun shone, and the wind was favourable.

On a round trip a favourable wind is one which is largely from behind on the return journey. This meant, of course, a head-wind for the first 40 miles.

Modern main roads, with long straights and great sweeping bends are not made for bicycles. There is nothing more dispiriting than grinding along some two mile stretch curving gently uphill into the wind with traffic roaring past. The Causewaymire doesn't have the traffic but it does have the long exposed straights. It can be exhilarating to bowl over the moors with a good following wind but is more often a slog, head down for mile after mile. So it was that morning,

At least in a car you are quickly past the ugly mess of the peat workings; on a bike you just cannot miss them. Then the scenery gradually improved with fine moorland vistas to the west; the larks were singing and the push into the wind became almost enjoyable. Slowly, slowly, Achavanich approached. Slowly, slowly, Loch Rangag passed below. I thought of the children who used to walk every day along this two mile stretch from the old poorhouse to the Achavanich school.

At last the Smerral turn, steeply downhill then winding through croft-lands to come out at the foot of Latheronwheel strath. It's well worth making the short detour to the old bridge, high above the wooded burn, a good place to stop for a bite to eat and a drink.

Back on the main road a large convoy of assorted army vehicles roared past and to get away from them I took the old road through the village, in any case a much better route to cycle. Although the old A9 above the castle is a dead-end for vehicles, you can get through on a bike. Many trees in the wood lay felled by recent January storms.

From Dunbeath to Berriedale is a hard stretch on a bike in a strong headwind, but eventually the fast descent to Berriedale appeared as another huge convoy of army vehicles started passing. A good excuse for another snack, watching them grind down the hill and even more slowly up the other side, very slow and steady as if tackling an Alpine pass. A few poor ordinary motorists were trapped behind the whole lot…

Berriedale is a place to linger, but the climb up the Ord on a bike is slow enough! Not half as bad as some of the north coast hills though. The 'soft escape bed' was closed for repairs (I've always wanted to dump a four-poster). Once up the hill the Ord gives an exhilarating ride, over the moors high above the sea, a road you hardly appreciate in a car.

A third army convoy was approaching from behind! Hurtling down to Helmsdale, pedalling as hard as I could, I just made it into the village ahead of them and turned up the peaceful Strath of Kildonan.

Perhaps the most amazing sight of the day was in Helmsdale station; a 12 coach train with two engines, modern coaches and sleepers. With that great 'Par-parp' which you rarely hear on the north line these days it chortled out and roared past me up towards Kinbrace, rich passengers no doubt peering from the windows for a glimpse of native kilts and bare feet.

What a difference a following wind makes to cycling! The 40 miles from Helmsdale to Melvich passed almost effortlessly, a delightful run. First through the lower wooded stretches of Kildonan then on through the sunlit bare clearance country, where salmon anglers thrashed the Kildonan. The traffic on the road consisted entirely of ghillies and keepers in 4 x 4's and the occasional angler's wife in something much flashier.

Cyclists often tour in groups, a nice social activity but a poor way of seeing the country. In such groups a pub or cafe stop seems obligatory but it always seems to me a shame to waste part of a day out by going into some stuffy hostelry! Lunch on my own by the river was much to be preferred, listening to the larks and gazing at the eternally flowing water. Then on, past Kinbrace and over the flows to Forsinard, on down through the crofts of Halladale.

A dose in the sun near Melvich revived me for the last 20 miles, over to suburban Reay then back into the clearance lands of Broubster. The glen seems even emptier without the old schoolhouse, so completely demolished that barely a trace remains.

Shoulders and arms were feeling tired more than the legs, but there was no hurry now, and the last few miles on familiar roads through the late afternoon sun were an enjoyable way of finishing the day. For some reason this round trip (or a very similar route) has been called 'The Hell of the North'. There could scarcely be a more inappropriate title – or did somebody do it in three-and-a half hours?

Breathing space

Where have I been over the last few weeks? Rushing about with little time to write articles and longing for a few quiet days in the hills! Nevertheless, in between escaping redundancy at work and various other minor events I've kept pedalling and enjoyed the odd magnificent day out.

A bit of fresh air and exercise pays off more than ever when things get, in the modern jargon, stressful. I had to travel south to report the previous year's work on a project which had just been axed by the English old-boys brigade so that it could be done in the South of England instead of the North of Scotland.

Might as well make the most of the opportunity to stop over a few days in Cumbria, I decided. Well, with depressing news on the radio, and signs of the recession all round, I'd reached a low ebb by the time I was queuing for the Penrith train out of Edinburgh Waverley station. Who should be there but a couple of friends who'd recently moved south from Caithness! Thus cheered, I wasn't too depressed later by the taxi-driver's stories of the soaring Penrith crime-rate.

Great to be back on a bike the next day, gales, rain and punctures notwithstanding. Pedalling up a 1700-foot pass feeling unworldly and half asleep, gradually waking up as the cloud turns into wind and rain. A slow puncture turned faster, I pumped up after 32 miles, then 16, then 8, then 4. A slow push up to the Tan Hill Inn, straight into the driving rain, new sheepskin mitts a lifesaver as that tyre needed pumping up every mile. The ride down was less exhilarating than usual and I finally gave up and walked the last two miles. Feeling better now, nothing like a February day's battle against the elements to restore perspectives!

Two days later, amazing brilliant sun with a couple of inches of snow, a bitter wind. Striding Dales weather! For anyone who is not physically disabled it can only be a tonic to step out for miles over the high Pennine moors on such a day.

Manchester didn't seem so bad after that, and though the meeting was a complete waste of time in the face of the 'anything north of Oxbridge is useless'

gang, at least I'd made something of the trip. Definitely the way to deal with business travel.

Suddenly, after months of pedalling back and forth in dark, it's light enough to take the lights off the bike and put them away till next October. The snipe are drumming in the early morning, larks are singing, lapwings displaying and the fair-weather cyclists are emerging from hibernation onto the Dounreay road. Funny that they all seem a lot faster than me, I surely should be super-fit having kept going through all the Winter storms! Maybe they've got the right idea. My running's been neglected too, and it took a postcard telling me that I'd got a place in this year's 'Highland Cross' biathlon to do something about it.

A glorious morning of early sun, with a slight ground-frost – ideal for a long run down one of those flow-country estate roads to a remote loch. Even though unfit, the run – or rather slow jog – was grand. There can be few better places to be than the heart of the Caithness flows on a fine morning, dark blue loch water lapping sandy beaches, the first golden plovers and redshanks calling, larks singing everywhere. Is this the same world that one hears about on the news? I walked half the way back, with a few blisters and stiff shoulders, but had at least managed my first ten miles of the year. Another great restorer of perspectives.

Some of the most content people in this world seem to be those who find solace in the hills and wild places, even though much of their lives may be hectic and difficult. Out-and-abouting has much to commend it!

Flow country hills

It must rank as one of the most obscure hills in Britain. Yet on a Caithness map one's eye is immediately drawn to a lump of high ground with a long name in the middle of the northern moors – Beinn Nam Bad Mor. It's not even 1000 feet high, but it's one of my favourites.

My first visit was on only my second day in the county; since then I've crossed it more often than any other Caithness peak except Olrig Hill. I was impressed then, as now, by the vast expanse of the northern flow country stretching to distant isolated peaks, by the glittering of dozens of lochs and lochans, by the old snowdrifts still lingering from the Winter blizzards.

As estate after estate has succumbed to the forestry the bare hilltop has become an island rising out of a sea of devastated peatlands to the north. The moors to the south are still untouched however, and the jewel of Loch Scye remains in the shallow corrie below the sister hill of Beinn Nam Bad Beg.

The easiest way to the hill is by the private track from Shurrery Lodge, more interesting, and longer, is via the track west of the Achvarasdal Burn from Reay. Much of this land used to be open but has now been afforested and the trees are slowly hiding the open space.

Three miles up the track from Reay is an old limekiln, two miles further on there's an old stables with fascinating graffiti dating back to the 1920s. After another heathery mile you have to cross the burn and skirt the new forest fence before picking your way across rough bogs to the barer, stony slopes overlooking Loch Scye. I've dragged a bike this way many times so don't complain!

The most interesting route is however to cross the moors from Broubster. On a Friday in early Spring I'd taken the Broubster road, with some misgivings, on the way home from work. It was a wild evening, getting dark, a north-westerly force seven and driving cold rain. The wind hurried me south, the rain sluicing off the road in sheets. Nobody now lives between Broubster cottage and Brawlbin;

a six mile stretch of road on which not to get a puncture in such conditions. It was as bleak and desolate as a Caithness road can be.

The wind dropped overnight and the rain cleared. At eight the next morning when I parked the car by the Forss bridge a fine dawn was just coming up with a thin skin of ice-crystals across the puddles and pools.

It's wellie country, particularly after rain; I splashed through the bogs beside the river to where the neighbouring forest fence curved away inland. This whole area is littered with grassy mounds, piles of stones, old ridges, furrows and walls, evidence of thousands of years of habitation which has only recently come to an end. My way led on across an area of dubh loch and bog to the Allt Forsiescye, straightened and enclosed in banks in centuries past. The banks may have preserved pasture then, but only preserve bog now, and the stream was hard to cross.

Then I came to Achforsiescye. The stream divides and runs down a short, steep slope in a series of slides and little waterfalls. In this isolated spot between the two falls are the ruins of a couple of old crofts, overlooking the lazybed ridges of a green field below. You could almost hear the lady of the house singing the old Gaelic songs as she went about her chores on such a fine early Spring morning while the children played by the burn. Now it's just a name on the map. It was a desperately hard life but we have lost much, with all our modern comforts and conveniences.

Another mile beyond the falls and over a moorland crest was Loch Scye, the sun dazzling off its blue-brown water as I picked my way round its northern shore. An easy climb of a few hundred feet led to the top of Beinn nam Bad Mor. The low sun was warm, the distant peaks hazy, the whole of the northern landscape silent, yet singing in the beauty of the Spring morning in Winter.

All that remained was to climb the fence half a mile to the north, pick my way across the churned up bog to the end of the forest road and stride the six miles back to the car. The best thing that can be said for this new road is that it gives a fast walk with some good views, though these will be hidden if the trees ever grow tall. The soft sandy surface was not making things easy for a mountain biker I met. In just 20 minutes drive I was back home for lunch – another world from Achforsiescye!

Signs of Spring

Spring comes fitfully here. However mild and sunny the weather may be now, we all know that blizzards and frosts will return, and it will be June before we can finally say goodbye to Winter.

Whatever the weather may do, the natural world is getting into gear for the summer, come downpour, blizzard or storm. Never mind the lambs, regarded by city people as synonymous with Spring. More intensive modern methods mean that their bleating can be heard at any time from Christmas onwards – and anyway Caithness farmers think only of the lambing storms followed by the May gobs.

Snowdrops are another matter. Nowhere else in Britain have I seen such displays as appear every year in the Olrig woods. In spite of the hard frosts the first white buds were showing at the end of January; growth continued slowly through a cold February to be at their most spectacular by the beginning of March.

Some of the real harbingers of spring are a little less romantic. The first squashed hedgehog on the road. The first large black slug venturing out across the garden. The first yellow flower of that pernicious weed, coltsfoot. The first spawning frogs, crowding muddy moorland pools, croaking, mating and fighting.

Rooks begin to prepare their nests in early March at Olrig, Ormlie and Braal. The first full song of a lark is usually heard in early February on a sunny day, and by March larks are singing everywhere except during the worst of weather. On the moors, the golden plovers are returning in February and March and once again the dubh lochs and bogs echo to their mournful calls.

On a mild evening at the end of February we heard the first snipe drumming from the hill, an evocative sound that will haunt the next few months. The odd peewit was out too, and a couple of weeks later others had joined in a dusk chorus with oystercatchers and curlews, all spurred into life by the lengthening daylight, whatever the weather may do.

Warm sunshine is hardly typical of Spring here, much more common are cold south-east winds, giving night after night of fighting the gales on the bike home from work. For me, Spring is really on the way when I get home by daylight and it's already half-light when I leave in the morning.

There came a brilliant, clear afternoon early in the month, with the late afternoon sun setting towards Ben Hope while Scaraben bore its characteristic white streaks below the three summits. Spring hills are streaked by the deep drifts accumulated in Winter blizzards and look quite different from when dusted by the first snows of Autumn. Then the fog came rolling in, first cutting off the top of distant Scaraben like an island above a white sea, then obscuring Spittal Hill and finally rolling in over Olrig to reduce the 50 mile view to Ben Hope to 50 yards. The next three days gave grey fog and drizzle – nothing more characteristic of a Caithness Spring than that!

By early April the sea birds will be returning to our cliffs to breed; already the fulmars have staked out claims and soon will come the kittiwakes, to be followed by guillemots, razorbills and shags, whatever the storms and gales may do. When the ammoniacal smell is drifting up from the geos, and the steep grass is almost hidden under the primrose and campion flowers, and the cliffs echo to the calls Kitt-ee-wake Kitt-ee-wake and cak-ackackackackack – and the fog drifts in and out across a sea intermittently dark blue and grey – then Spring is really here.

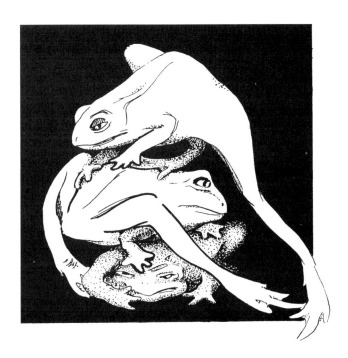

Eribol and Olrig

Caithness often experiences a long spell of cold grey east winds in early Spring and this year has been no exception. I thought we'd got away with it until, three weeks ago, the south-east wind strengthened all day and was gusting to force nine by mid-afternoon. It took nearly two hours to cycle the 15 miles home from work and there's hardly been an evening since without a head-wind! Its been dreich lambing weather and many two-week-old lambs must have had quite a shock on the first sunny day. Ever-optimistic, the larks and curlews go on singing.

On a particularly bleak Easter Saturday morning of driving rain I drove westwards, early. Often when the wind is south-easterly Caithness is much wetter than places just a few miles further west and so it was this time, by Reay it was only drizzling and once west of Bettyhill the roads and ground were dry.

Easter Saturday, 55 miles drive – and I think I met one car. Not the least of the many advantages of living in the Far North! Leaving the car near the end of the road past Melness I set off on foot up the track leading towards Ben Hutig. Although dry, a bitter east wind blew and the grey cloud lowered from time to time to the top of Hutig. After a mile or so this new, expensively bulldozed track ends for no particular reason above a small loch. A sign attached to a gatepost warns people to watch out for drug traffickers! The out-of-the-way beaches around here obviously have attractions for another kind of person altogether.

Another hour and the top of Ben Hutig, only 1350 feet high but a superb viewpoint for the Kyle of Tongue and Loch Eribol. Some small, very solidly built drystone enclosures have always puzzled me – a First World War lookout, perhaps?

Without going into too much detail over the rest of my route I can say that it led along the finest cliff scenery in the North, with at one point a view vertically down a 600-foot cliff to an inaccessible bay, packed almost solid with basking seals. Some of the cliffs further east are virtually unvisited, as witnessed by a

boulder, bristling with garnets, which would have been removed in more fre-
quented parts. A small stream tumbled down a waterfall into a little ravine, overgrown with stunted birch and alder. One felt that this spot would be one of the
few forever unaffected by man's activities. Never a footprint, never a sweetie
paper!

Following clifftops demands determination not to make shortcuts, and provides ample rewards in views of hidden stacks, waterfalls and rocky bays. Even I
cut the corners though on the last half mile to Strathan Bay, avoiding three steep
ups and downs at the end of the day. A lazy stroll across half a mile of sands and
a wander up the Melness Burn took me back to the car.

The grey, cold winds continued. A couple of days later, in temperatures of four
degrees Celsius which would have been reasonable in January, never mind April,
I set off beneath leaden skies for a local run. Grey and cold indeed over Olrig Hill
with the ground, normally dry at this time of year, still saturated. Low cloud was
brushing over the tops of the masts. On, down the roads to Murkle, down the
track to the grey sands of Murkle Bay. Little visited, this spot deserves to be

better known, though suffering from a tendency to collect rotting weed. The low slabby rocks from here to Castletown boast rockpools and seaweeds the equal of any.

Low cliffs led me round the headland to the little bay of West Murkle, there then followed a long, slow jog up the road, straight into the bitter wind. A track carries straight on, across the main road, leading into a bowl of farmland below Sibmister and a steep climb up the ski slopes to the Weydale Quarries. At the back of these is the old quarry face, a quarter of a mile long, which anywhere else would be prized as a practice ground for rock-climbers. Beyond is the roughest and wettest part of Olrig Hill, a haven for curlews, snipe, grouse, lapwings, redshanks, and larks. Good to get back home after a ten-mile run on a day which would have been cold for December!

Cold weather notwithstanding, Spring advances. The cliff-nesting birds are here. Coastal slopes are bright with primroses, marshes are yellow with marsh-marigold. Violets are out, pussy willows are on the trees, the larches are showing green. Get out and see, before you miss it and find its suddenly Summer!

My own back yard

If asked what my 'hobby' is I'm always a bit stuck for an answer – but would like to say 'exploring'. The trouble is that this conjures up images of the Venezuelan plateaux, or the Greenland Ice-Cap, places I'd love to explore but somehow doubt that I ever will. No, for me, exploring means – well – I suppose getting to know the area around where I find myself.

You can't go exploring by car. If you are an invalid or infirm, and have no other means of getting about, seeing the country from a car is certainly a lot better than sitting at home. But if anyone with usable legs and eyes tells me they've explored somewhere and have merely driven around by car with perhaps the odd half-hour stop, then I keep a tactful silence. In my opinion they might have done almost as well by staying at home and studying the map.

As a child I used to walk home from the bus-stop with some others who would disappear off down a little side passage between houses. It never occurred to me to wonder where the passage went till one evening, at the age of about 13 when I was getting bored watching the telly. There and then I got up, walked down the road and went down that passage for the first time in my life. I still remember that sort of surprised delight which greets the explorer of the unknown when I discovered that it came out at the end of a cul-de-sac I'd never visited, which then led out into a well-known street.

From then on I never looked back; many evenings were spent walking miles exploring little paths, back alleys, canal banks, old railway tracks, abandoned quarries. There were surprising oases of woodland, fields and hilltops, there were even streams and a waterfall hidden in the most unlikely spot in the middle of a housing estate It was an area which abounded in nooks and crannies; I would do an eight mile round walk to explore some little path made by local children around the back of a few houses. By the time I was 18 and left that part of the world I knew every inch of the area within five miles of the house.

I spent six years in the far North of England with the Northern Pennines nearby; every Saturday I'd set off early on a series of bus rides into the dales with a walk on my own of 15–35 miles across the moors to another bus ride home. Once again it was the unknown that fascinated, I had to climb all the hills, walk all the watersheds, explore all the little valleys, take all the routes through the forest. I reckoned I'd walked at least once (and often many times) through almost every kilometre square on a couple of Ordnance Survey maps by the time I left the area.

It is so much part of me to get to know my own surroundings that I find it hard to understand people who haven't done as much as even visit the well-known places nearby or drive the side roads by car. There will always be somewhere one hasn't managed to visit – but how can anyone drive down the A9 (say) without at least the urge to stop and walk up the glens and hills, or along the clifftops or down to the harbours, or round the lochs.

The Highlands are vast, you'll never get to know them, but you can at least make the most of every opportunity! There is so, so much when you go looking. To take a typical example; have you ever stopped, on the way north, to climb the hill above Loch Migdale, near Bonar Bridge?

Loch Migdale is a beautiful spot (not a beauty spot!) with woods rising up into the great cliffs of the Rock overlooking the loch. Yes, it took me years to get round to visiting the top of Migdale Rock but there have been so many other places to visit! All I can say is – get the map out, turn off at Bonar Bridge and have a walk along Loch Migdale. If you manage to get to the hilltop above you'll find deep heather, no path, a fine view and an old cairn which appears to have been unvisited in the last 50 years. The hill's only 750 feet high and no more than three miles from Bonar Bridge so presumably few explorers live there. They've probably all gone to Canada or New Zealand – or perhaps even Venezuela.

The hills are alive

Music has a strange capacity for forming associations. I confess to being more ignorant and less interested in music than most people, but suffer from getting tunes stuck in the head, going round and round, sometimes taking days to exorcise. They may be pop, dance, hymn tunes or just some silly rhythm, probably not even anything I like. Meanwhile the associations build up and, oddly, these are almost always connected with the hills.

Old tunes bring back old memories. Signature tunes of TV programmes from 30 years ago have an instant capacity for evoking some Lake District mountain, or a rocky hill river in North Wales. One, from a program I never even watched ('Boy meets Girl' I think it was called) transports me to Creag Meagaidh above Laggan, late afternoon after a day of wind and rain, emerging from cloud to the vast grey emptiness of upper Glen Roy and a bothy night ahead.

Pop tunes, forced into my ears on the daily school bus, have all sorts of places connected with them. One immediately brings to mind a magnificent February half-term Youth Hostelling trip, sunshine and hills covered in deep soft snow. Another ('there's a hole in my shoe, and it's letting in water... ') conjures up a long walk down a disused railway in a thundery downpour at the age of 15. A song about ships brings to mind not the sea, but a first Youth Hostel trip, walking 20 miles with the sort of fluey cold that would now send me to bed.

Simon and Garfunkel singing 'Strawberry Fair' – and I'm transported to an evening train across Rannoch Moor, the low sun glowing on the Blackmount and Mamores, a long day's walk from Killin to Bridge of Orchy behind, Loch Ossian Hostel ahead. 'Homeward Bound' perhaps more rationally associates with the last, and longest, miles to to a hostel or bothy, in particular the now closed Strathtummel hostel and the 27 mile walk thereto via Glen Tilt from Inverey. This used to be a well-known challenge as the longest walk given in the SYHA handbook!

'Tea for two' (these things are quite random) brings to mind the Caithness marathon and must be a good jogging tune! Tunes, hummed to oneself, are often useful in providing rhythm for running or for a long, steady climb (Do people use Walkmans now?) One such, four hands on a piano, I first used 30 years ago and still do, occasionally. To this day it brings to mind a now long-demolished hostel at a remote spot in North Wales where I first heard it played by two nice girls from the Wirral!

How many times have I set off alone into the grey dawn, a long journey by public transport, a long walk over empty hills in uncertain winter weather! The tune 'In the early morning rain' (and I know neither the words nor who sung it) brings to mind countless such occasions, particularly in the bleakest parts of the Northern Pennines. Early morning signature tunes on the radio likewise bring back many long days, a 'Good Morning Wales' tune, long since abandoned by the BBC, makes me think of the Black Mountains of South Wales (or is it the other way round?). The old Radio Scotland tune comes to mind when cycling home from work on any wild winter night of squally showers.

Tunes have to be catchy to stick, so the great classical works have no associations at all. The vast majority of hymn tunes were ruined by frequent use at school or are too boring to remember, though some of the more lively modern ones do have associations. One brings to mind Boblainy Forest, long runs through heat and insects in the early morning, hidden waterfalls and far moorland summits. Another makes me think of the remotest Affric tops, a long climb with full camping gear up the peaks north of Mam Soul and a late evening run across one of the high tops north of Strathfarrar.

Scottish Country Dance tunes I like, and the dancing too, provided both are lively and not too complicated! One tune takes me to the Galloway Hills, the Merrick and Mullwharchar on a bitter April day of wind and snow-showers, of newspaper stuffed in the roof of Tunskeen bothy to stop the snow blowing in through a hole. Another makes me think immediately of the the North train, wending its ways up long Kildonan Strath and over the moors to Altnabreac on a dark stormy night.

'Mairie's Wedding', a favourite tune and dance, is also linked with an April day. This however was a day of scorching heat and clear air, a miraculous day, one of a week of continuous sunshine on a camping trek across Sutherland. I was on the Meall Horn range, slowly crossing the summits after camping on Arkle, a day which ended by Loch an Dherue below Ben Loyal. The memories of aching shoulders, of thirst, of sore feet have gone, the memories of light and sun, the freedom of remotest north-west Sutherland for a whole miraculous week will remain for the rest of my life.

The hills are indeed alive with the sound of music though not, at any rate for me, the sort of music you might expect!

From Kildonan to Berriedale

The vast majority of hill-walkers drive a car to the foot of their chosen peaks. Cars insulate you from the environment, you reach some remote spot without appreciating the gradual transition from settlement to mountain. Walking from buses or trains usually means walking from one inhabited area across the hills to another, which is much more satisfying.

On a frosty Saturday in early April I joined the 6AM train out of Thurso to travel to Kildonan. It always seems strange to catch this train when not bound for a journey of hundreds of miles! Many of the long-distance travellers that morning must have looked out with some surprise at the passenger alighting at 7.15 on the snow-dusted Kildonan platform.

The train rattled off southwards and the silence of the early morning hills descended. A few birds sung, optimistically, from the bare wet birches, hazy snow-shower clouds clung to the higher slopes. My aim was to cross the hills to Berriedale, taking in a number of peaks, weather permitting. Strong west winds were forecast (from behind, another advantage of A to B walking) with heavy snow-showers likely. At Berriedale I'd catch a bus back to Thurso.

Early snow-showers had already left a covering of half an inch. Still not fully awake, I wended my way slowly along sheep tracks above the Kildonan Burn to pick up a path which climbed steadily up the moorland slopes of Cnoc Salislade. It didn't matter being slow, there was all day, I could take my time. The freedom of the hills! The wind gradually picked up, lifting cloud off the rounded moorland tops. To the north-west could be seen the very white outline of Ben Armine and to the south, the steep slopes of Ben Uarie with cloud obstinately clinging.

With the low sun and bitter wind it could have been January – but in April it always warms up and becomes more Spring-like as the day goes on. An icy snow shower drove in on Cnoc Salislade, clearing to sun on the saddle to the next, higher top of Creag Nan Gearr.

The Langwell Water has its source here at Loch Scalabsdale, the highest loch in the county and I left the pack here for a quick jog up and down the third highest top in the county, Creag Scalabsdale. Large patches of old frozen snow remained, it had been a long, snowy Winter in the hills. As the next shower drove in from the west I climbed up to the little rocky tor of 'The Child's Seat'; there are some good stone shelters just below the top and here I enjoyed a bite to eat watching the snow blow harmlessly past.

The uppermost reach of the Langwell Water is a grand remote spot, overlooked by Morven and rarely visited. A couple of miles down the valley are the remains of a prehistoric 'wheelhouse', on a rise with a stunning view all round. There was still enough shelter to eat lunch out of the wind, the sun now hot. The valley from here, down to Berriedale, may have been inhabited for 5000 years until the clearances, just 150 years ago.

The track down to Berriedale makes a long, pleasant amble, however I preferred to take the mountain route. With the wind strengthening from behind and the air cold and clear, it was an exhilarating climb up over Sal-Vaich, descending to a col which was once a well-used route from Berriedale to Braemore. An old slab bridge over one of the hill burns still remains.

The climb onto Scaraben was steep, then the familiar quartzite summit ridge. There can be few days when a gale isn't blowing here, and this Winter the temperature will have hardly ever risen above freezing. The short heather was completely brown and dead-looking between the scree and banks of frozen snow. The view was of that mix of dark-blues and browns and whites so characteristic of early Spring.

The wind was still rising, and showers moving in from the west as I picked my way carefully down the southern slopes to follow a burn which descended towards the Berriedale Water. Large herds of deer moved off, slowly. Sleet and snow swept in. It seemed a long, rough descent by a fine hill stream with an unexpected waterfall. At last, the Langwell track and easy walking.

With plenty of time before my bus I enjoyed pottering the last couple of miles down through the estate wood to Berriedale. It is a great shame that the garden centre here has closed, it always made an excellent day out, particularly with small children. Now it all looks off-puttingly private, though there's nothing to stop you walking up the road through the woods. I crossed the main road and carried on down to the little harbour; already the first kittiwakes were on the cliff above the mouth of the Berriedale Water. This is perhaps the best place in the county to see them at close range.

One of the problems with taking a car is the long drive home when you're already tired after a hard day. Much better to relax on the bus, look out at the views, and let the driver do the concentrating!

Easter in the Cairngorms

It's snowing hard again, rattling on the tent flysheet. The Primus is roaring, heating up a steamed pudding. Damp clothes in the tent entrance are steaming gently, inside I'm warm and dry. Down in Braemar the coach parties are settling into the Fife Arms Hotel, B&B's are opening up, Youth Hostellers are cooking meals in the steamy hostel kitchen. I wouldn't be anywhere else but here.

It always seems to snow when I go the Cairngorms, even in June, though it's hardly unexpected in mid-April. Yet it had been so mild on the day I drove down, wet till Inverness then bleak and grey over the vast snow-streaked Grampians by Tomintoul to Braemar.

Linn of Dee and Derry Lodge are hallowed ground for generations of hill-goers. One hears so much about this area that you almost forget it's a real place. A huge new carpark (tastefully screened) surprised me; things have changed in the 25 years since I last walked from Loch Morlich over Ben Macdhui to Inverey Youth Hostel. Here is Mar Lodge, rebuilt at great expense, with the estate recently sold for six million to the National trust for Scotland.

Taking the bike down from the car roof and precariously balancing the pack on the carrier, I pedalled off up the bumpy track to Derry Lodge. This is a favourite route for mountain bikers, yet my battered old road bike coped reasonably well. The lodge is now uninhabited, as are an increasing number of remoter Highland dwellings, and the windows are boarded up. Tents were scattered liberally among the old Scots pines where the Derry and Luibeg rivers join, and there was even a public telephone. A sort of advanced base camp.

For once I was unashamedly bagging Munros, and took the opportunity to nip up Beinn Bhreac, perhaps an uninspiring peak to many but indeed a fine Grampian top overlooking great expanses of gravelly plateau and moor, home of the ptarmigan and arctic hare, blasted by gales and scorched by sun. Then back down to camp in seclusion a couple of miles further on near Luibeg Bridge, just off the Lairig Ghru path.

The many stands of fine Scots Pine are a feature of this country, and it was encouraging to see that several areas had been fenced to keep out the deer and allow natural regeneration of seedlings which are otherwise all eaten. Encourage the right trees in the right places!

The morrow was a day of hills, in increasingly cold winds and showers which gave snow down to the tent by evening with a hard frost following. Shortly after midnight I looked outside. The sky was mostly cloudy but moonlight glimmered on the vast landscape of mountains dusted and streaked with snow. There seemed something menacing about the scene. I remembered then that Ben Macdhui, reputedly haunted by the evil 'Grey Man' rose straight above me. The crowds have certainly driven any haunting away in summer but alone, at night, that peak has a funny feel to it. Much tougher climbers than I have had frightening experiences there. I scuttled back into the tent feeling like a child hiding under the bedclothes!

Having the use of a car tempted me to the Cairnwell on the next day, for a few easy Munros above the highest British main road, at 2200 feet. I had not realised that this was the Glenshee ski centre, and of all the Scottish centres, the worst mess. The trouble with Scottish skiing is that the mountains are ruined for much of the year for the sake of (perhaps) 40 days skiing. Every slope down to the pass is disfigured by tows and lifts and the top of the pass is one gigantic carpark. What a shame that a few portable tows run by enthusiastic amateurs had to come to this. Here's to no more expansion of commercial skiing in Scotland! I suspect global warming will close it all down in a few years anyway. I just hope they clear up the mess.

Depressed, I chose a more conventional outing (for me) today and enjoyed it in spite of dreadful weather. Snow showers on an east wind had already started as I pedalled through Braemar and up the three miles of gravelly track to Lochcallater Lodge. Boarded up and disused again, this lodge had a magnificent setting under the hills by a high loch.

From the lodge a path leads for six miles to Lochnagar, a famous peak on which I'd never set foot. There was also the chance to traverse the delightfully named Carn an t-Sagairt Mor (actually just a rounded high hump). As I gained height the snow came on harder, first pellets, then flakes, then fine blowing drift. Three miles of the route lay at over 3000 feet, and over the plateau I trudged, into weather that was turning into a blizzard. By the time I reached the summit, conditions were nearing whiteout, there was nothing to see of the tremendous cliffs except the edge, and that to keep well clear of.

Without the compass I would, literally, have been lost finding my way down. There are few occasions when you need to use it but when you do, you really do!

Big white flakes were falling hard even down by Loch Callater, and it was a lovely walk back along the shore in gently falling rather than wildly blowing snow. Even in Braemar it was turning thick, to the disconsolation of the coach parties. It is as well to remember that April is still Winter in the highlands.

A couple of miles walk took me back to the tent, in a sheltered spot on the edge of a wood high above the River Dee. Good, that pudding's done now. I think I've earned half a tin of cream to go with it!

Training

The thought of seizing up with cramp half way down Glen Affric provides a wonderful stimulus for building up the jogging miles! In only two months time I'm going to have to run 20 miles over rough mountain tracks from Kintail to Affric in the annual 'Highland Cross' and then race another 30 by bike to Beauly. The trouble is that, as usual, I've left things a bit late...

My first longer run this year was from the unlikely starting point of Balmoral, indeed just half a mile from the castle. Mid-April blizzards which had blocked some of the higher roads were interspersed with brilliant sunshine. All the huge carparks were completely empty, as was a little pull-in just opposite the entrance to Balmoral village itself. Here, as the snow whirled past again I donned my faithful running shoes, stuffed a bit of spare clothing and a banana into a poly bag and jogged off into the wind.

Just four miles from Balmoral lies Gelder Shiel, one of the royal picnic spots. Here too is one of the famous bothies, formerly a stables and now, by royal decree, equipped with hard wooden bunks and a table. There is no fire, it's a bleak place indeed in wintry weather and is mostly used by hard-bitten rock-climbers bound for Lochnagar. It made, however, a nice objective for a morning run.

The snow was coming down thickly as I jogged slowly along the track leading up through the pine forests. Once out in the open, the wind was bitter, but the sky cleared and the sun came out, brilliant on the open moor.

Down the track towards me, weaving about through the snow, came three cyclists, heavily wrapped up in balaclavas and capes. As they passed me, the third, a lady, commented that evidently they weren't the only lunatics abroad that morning. The same thought had occurred to me. They'd have had a cold night in the bothy!

Slowly the clump of trees marking Gelder Shiel drew nearer, as did, from behind, black clouds looking like the end of the world. Ahead, cloud from the

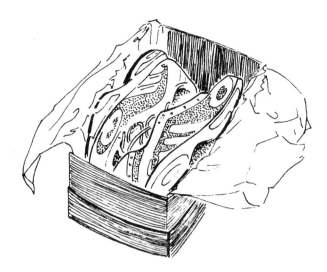

last shower was just clearing the dazzling white summit of Lochnagar which I had struggled up to, in a blizzard, the day before.

The bothy was damp and cold. I quickly munched a banana, donned light cagoule and overtrousers and headed back towards Balmoral as snow pellets rattled down, quickly turning to thick white flakes. It was a slow, head-down into-the-wind two miles until the snow-shower turned back to bright sunshine. The partly-covered tracks of three bicycles and some idiot on foot led me back to the village.

Back in Caithness a few days later and a longer run across the flow country. My route followed a trail for seven miles to a moorland loch then, passing through some of the least visited country in the county, took a boggy little glen to a second loch and continued down a long winding river. After many miles jogging I was ready to walk a bit – but that wind, now gale-force, was bitterly cold and the first of several increasingly violent showers rattled down. The outing was proving tougher than planned. Walking fast, fortunately with the wind from behind and with all my scanty spare clothing on, I just about kept warm. There was no way I was running all the way, but after three miles walk and a crossing of some dubh loch country I reached the next loch and a good track for jogging. The wind blew me along at a good pace for the next four miles, accompanied for a time by driving sleet, then I had to cut across country again, sideways on to the wind. It was only another two miles hard going, showered by spray from sizable waves breaking against the loch shore, before at last I reached that welcome change of dry clothes and flask of tea back at the car.

Conditions on the Highland Cross can range from scorching sun to cold driving rain. I should at any rate be well prepared for the latter!

Explore Caithness

Caithness is a land of surprises. Many a visitor, whisked by car from Wick airport to Dounreay and back, has taken away an impression of flat, boring, almost treeless farmland with a few bits of barren moorland and an uninviting rocky coast.

'I HATE that journey!' is a not uncommon comment on the train ride across the county from Forsinard. When enthusing about this stretch of line – the Autumn colours, the deer, the low sunlight on the hills and lochans, the cloudscapes – I've been regarded with some amazement ' But there's absolutely NOTHING there – just one stunted tree!'

But just go and look. Potter around. Wander the clifftops. Scramble down the geos. Peer into the old ruins. Follow moorland burns through chains of lochs to their sources. Explore the old quarries. Walk across the county away from the roads and realise how fragile is man's grip on this exposed northern land. Visit the standing stones – and find on the way many once standing, now fallen – and the brochs and the cairns and the castles. Caithness reveals a mass of interest and beauty once you look below the superficial surface appearance.

Just a couple of examples. Take a stretch of the A9 a few miles south of Wick, running through ordinary coastal farmland north of Clyth. Stop at the bend at Bruan and you'll find that the road here is right on the clifftop with an unsuspected 300-foot drop into the sea. Have a look at the derelict church with behind it a large, spectacularly collapsed concrete barn, destroyed in some past storm. Just 200 yards north is the track of the old Lybster railway which gives a pleasant walk for a mile to Loch Watenen, a place quite unsuspected from the main road. The area behind the loch is one of the richest in the county for standing stones, chambered cairns and brochs.

Just across the main road are the famous, but unsignposted, Whaligoe steps; over 300 of them up which women carried baskets of herring from the little harbour at the bottom of the geo. Fine contorted cliffs run north-east for a mile to Ulbster where a waterfall tumbles into the sea below the deserted Mains. At the farm is an old graveyard and a family tomb building with a very fine circular slated roof. And so on, the more you look the more you see – typical Caithness.

Walk out from Loch More, following the new fence, on a track which passes the old croft of Balvreed. The track gets lost in bogs but persevere for another mile deeper into the moor and you'll arrive at a long low building overlooking the moorland Loch Thulachan. No mere abandoned croft this, an entire old lodge of some fifteen rooms falling gradually into decay, with rotting floorboards, broken windows and loose roof sheets. There are still baths and WCs and the remains of a hot water system, still an old cooker, piles of broken plates, disintegrating beds and cupboards. A somewhat disquieting hangover from a past age, now forgotten and left to moulder back into the moors in the middle of nowhere.

Again typically Caithness. The whole county is full of nooks and crannies and interest, most not at all well known. There are lots of discoveries to be made, new species to name, unknown antiquities to find, old paths and drove roads to uncover, the list goes on. Explore your own backyard and never mind the foreign holidays!

Easter weather

Change and contrast. That, perhaps, is what makes the climate, or rather climates, so delightfully interesting in Caithness and the Highlands.

Spring had seemingly arrived on Easter Sunday with warm sun, birdsong and the daffodil buds starting to open; on Monday a mild and gentle breeze blew from the south. The next morning was bright and clear, but the wind had swung into the north and the fibrous-white shower clouds were piled high and beginning to sweep in.

Much of the snow had melted from Ben Loyal and Ben Hope but large streaks and patches were still evident as I drove west. The wind was strong and cold at the foot of Loyal; higher up occasional flurries of sleet and hail swept across the slopes. My route was simple; up to the north top, along the ridge to the summit then back down. The eastern slopes were fairly sheltered from the strong, gusty wind and, surprisingly, it was quite calm on the north top with the gale deflected by the steep slopes.

A shower was coming in as I stood on the high, rocky perch above precipitous slopes falling for over 2000 feet, with the Kyle of Tongue beyond. Streamers of hail and snow started to twist and writhe across the mountainside.

A great golden eagle came soaring round the corner, a couple of hundred yards away, having perhaps glided the length of the western slopes. Have you ever seen an eagle jump? This one did; its wings twitched in a quick flutter before it soared on, trying to look unconcerned at the unexpected figure standing on its favourite lookout.

I drove south the next day, into a real West Highland deluge of sheeting rain at Loch Arkaig. A five mile jog up into the hills left me as wet as if I'd been for a swim in the loch with my track-suit on...

Three days later and the heat-haze had set in. I was climbing a craggy, boulder-strewn peak north of Strathcarron and comfortable wearing shorts and a T-shirt even at 2000 feet. A cool breeze demanded a pullover on the very top, but it was warm enough to linger over lunch enjoying the panorama of snow-streaked peaks shimmering in the heat. The descent was hot and dusty with the few remaining snow-patches visibly shrinking. Beside the Dingwall road, old ladies were sitting outside their cottages taking tea in the warm late afternoon sun.

At nine the next morning, little over 12 hours later, the weather looked much the same – hazy, bright, just a little cloud on the tops. But when I stepped out of the car near the Crask Inn it was into a bitter easterly near-gale far colder than it had been at 3000 feet on the previous day.

The route up Ben Klibreck from the west is never a very interesting walk and on that day was little better than a slog. It took, seemingly, hours of head-down push into that howling wind to reach the south ridge which was being swept by a gale of 70–100 MPH. If there hadn't been one or two others battling their way on towards the summit I'd probably have turned back; as it was it took a staggering, drunken near-crawl to get along the ridge and up the last 500 feet of hoar-covered slopes to the top.

The remaining snow was frozen rock-hard, long frost feathers adorned the higher rocks and I was completely wrapped up in warm clothes with even my face covered by hood and ski-goggles. The previous day's bare arms and sun hat at the same altitude seemed more than vaguely impossible.

The next week at home remained grey and cold. A fortnight after Easter and the daffodils in the garden were still just beginning to come out…

Across Assynt

The night in the bothy had been cold and the ground was white with early frost in the calm of the dawn. The ramparts of Suilven were already glowing in early sun beneath a clear sky, it looked like the day might turn hot. I stuffed my sunhat into a pocket and set off, pack on back, along the path towards Assynt.

For an hour I ambled up through the serene peace of the sunlit glen below Suilven and Canisp until a low-flying jet screamed out of the east marking a change in the style of the day. My way now led up the steep and rugged pathway towards Canisp, a slow climb carrying a full camping rucksac but shaded from the sun by rapidly growing bubbly white clouds.

Gradually the lochan-strewn landscape of Sutherland sank below me as I scrambled up the summit ridge to the top where patchy snow still lay. Canisp is a good vantage point for the rugged country of West Sutherland with over a hundred lochs visible, some now ominously dark below steadily growing clouds. My route ahead looked a long one, down to the Inchnadamph road then up across the Breabag spur of Ben More Assynt.

The eastern side of Canisp is gentler and gave an easy, steady descent of three or four miles to the road, but with an ominous shower of cold hail. The lower slopes of Ben More Assynt are, incongruously, limestone country more reminiscent of the Yorkshire Dales than the Highlands. There are white rocks, rounded and hollowed as if sculpted, there are dry grassy meadows and rivers running underground leaving empty bouldery beds. The glen leading up to Breabag however seemed endless and at three in the afternoon with a steep climb of 1000 feet ahead it was very tempting to stop and spend the rest of the day pottering about in the sun and looking at the nearby caves.

This 'Lotus Eaters' syndrome is familiar to hill campers and in fact it was likely that, by the time the tent was up, the sun would have vanished and I'd have to spend the rest of the day sitting watching the rain, with the prospect of a marathon walk on the next day.

So, resolutely I pushed on up the steep slopes, tired and slow, but at last getting back into the high hill country of moss, lichen, and snow patches with the golden plover piping mournfully. The sun had indeed now gone and the weather looked ominous, but it was still dry.

Nine hours after leaving the bothy I stood on the edge of a three mile long tier of broken cliffs with the upper reach of the River Oykel, where I had hoped to camp that night, 1200 feet below. There was no obvious way down.

A shower was moving in from the east; it didn't look much as Loch Shin was still visible through the grey veils of hail and rain. I started walking along the cliff tops in the first of the hail looking for a good place to pitch the tent and noticed a steep but just possible route of descent, linking up grassy and heathery rakes between crags. I started down. The hail was now heavy and the steep slopes were rapidly turning a slippery white as I picked my way gingerly on. The first hopeful route ended above crags; I had to climb back up and try another with all the time the hail making balancing on the 60-degree slopes with a heavy rucsac more and more tricky. At last I reached the top of the steep heathery rake I'd been aiming for which ran out without difficulty into the peatbogs below.

By the time I'd reached the river Oykel steady, heavy, cold rain was falling, the ground was saturated and covered in half-melted hail. Camping conditions are never ideal in the Highlands but the worse the weather, the greater the satisfaction of sitting dry in the tent cooking a meal!

The light shower lasted four hours and my sunhat was still, soggily, in my pocket.

Waist-deep snow

A day's walk in the Highlands can easily turn into an expedition, particularly in the Winter or the wet.

After a night of heavy rain on melting snow, just after Easter, the water was pouring off the hills around the Great Glen. Rather than risk being cut off by floods at the end of Loch Arkaig, where I'd planned to go, I'd opted for the comfort of the Loch Lochy Youth Hostel.

The weather had improved by morning, into that typical mountain 'sunblink and drizzle' weather; warm and muggy in the glens, but with cloud, intermittent rain and blowing drizzle over the hills. The odd patch of blue sky or gleam of sun makes you think that it's clearing but the drizzle always returns.

Instead of aiming for the higher peaks on such a day it seemed a nice idea to walk across rather lower hills to Glen Roy, to visit a bothy at the head of the glen, then return by a different route.

The sides of the Great Glen have largely been afforested, clear-felled and re-planted. Without an up-to-date map to show the forest roads and rides I was soon in trouble, trying to find a way through Sitka thickets on steep slopes with tantalising easy ground on the other side of a burn in spate which couldn't be crossed.

The forest had collected snow in recent blizzards and great wet patches had to be wallowed through and up in the muggy warmth and drizzle. Eventually I found my way out and picked my way through bog and slush to arrive at a bleak peaty col above Glen Turret. Two miles covered, two hours taken.

Even up here the youthful burn, rushing down towards Glen Turret, was hard to cross; a mile downstream it was a roaring torrent. Another burn came in from the side, on the map it was just a short line of the thinnest blue, but if there hadn't been a narrows where I could leap across the spate I'd have had to turn back.

A shaky bridge crossed the next burn and at last I was down into Glen Roy with easy going on paths and tracks. The sun appeared, the rain stopped and for the next five miles I strode out up the glen, thoroughly enjoying the walk. High, rolling mountains, streaked with snow and capped with cloud and drizzle rose all round. The River Roy thundered down in full spate; everywhere that ever ran with water was running with water.

The famous 'parallel roads' of Glen Roy are shorelines of a loch which filled the Glen at the end of the last Ice Age, each 'road' marking a level of the loch. They do not, unfortunately, provide easy walking over rough country and only appear to look like roads from a distance, snaking around hillsides on the same contour line.

Lunch was eaten in the bothy, out of the wind, before setting off on a different route back over the hills to the Great Glen. I say hills. The peaks between here and Loch Lochy rise to 2600 feet; with so many higher peaks around one tends to belittle them. They are however real mountains, rugged, rough and wild and to be treated with respect.

Just a mile up from the bothy the corry opened out into a morass of peat. The hollows between the peat hummocks were filled with deep wet snow in which I wallowed, waist deep. The weather was deteriorating, cloud was coming down and the wind blew the rain in sheets across the desolate landscape. Straight into the wind and rain, across that atrocious terrain for further than I could see, lay my planned route. The walk had become an expedition.

There was no real cause for concern. The weather was mild, I was well equipped, fit, with plenty of food and hours of daylight. It was just a question of slowly, carefully, carrying on. First I went down to the river, in impressive spate, seeking better going along its banks. It was easier, though still necessary to do a fair bit of climbing up and down, wading through more deep slushy snowdrifts, taking care where the banks were under water or where there was a risk of slipping into the river – and never getting out.

After another mile the going improved and soon I was traversing the grassy, almost snow-free flanks of Carn Dearg, climbing up into the cloud.

My route now led on across the complex high peatlands around the headwaters of the River Turret. It was quite simple – just take a compass bearing and walk in a straight line for three miles. The going was however not of the best – islands of peat rising out of deep melting snow, possibly concealing hidden burns. Sometimes it was possible to jump across between the 'islands', sometimes the snow would start off only knee deep then I'd be in up to the waist for a strenuous wallow out onto the other side.

Cloud and rain came and went almost unnoticed, any clearance just revealing more of the endless, desolate landscape. Tempting valleys curved down to the left – the wrong direction. The compass is always correct!

All things come to an end at last. A gentle crest was gained, revealing a deep valley cutting off to the north-west and all that I had to do now was go down.

Soon I was into the forest, cutting across cleared hillsides into growing warmth and sunshine. Almost before I knew it the Spring had returned, with primroses in flower and young families out for a walk along the path. That snowy, peaty plateau had not been so remote and endless after all. It only felt like it.

A flow country walk

The moors of Caithness must be one of the least-known areas of Britain, almost unvisited other than by stalkers and fishermen. A first impression is usually of miles of flat featureless boggy nothing, with a few inhospitable black lochans, exposed to all the violence of the elements. The truth about the moorland, or flow country as it is now known, is rather different.

On a fine day in late May or June you stride down the track under the big sky, the distant high peaks of Caithness and Sutherland sharp in the crystal air on the far moorland rim. Larks rise and golden plovers pipe mournfully from tussocks. A herd of deer scatters, perhaps some of the hinds with new calves; you see deer all day and realise how common they are away from human habitation.

Near the end of the track is an old house; the panelling inside bears signatures dating back to 1900 from stalkers, keepers and fishermen and is embellished with poems, drawings of deer and tallies of fish caught. A little further on is the first real moorland loch, nearly encircled by white sandy beaches marked only by the footprints of deer and otters. The peaty water reflects that particular brilliant dark blue which is such a feature of our northern Summers. A red-breasted merganser flaps off to draw your attention away from her eight chicks splashing rapidly in the opposite direction, an osprey may be seen diving for fish and sometimes, effortlessly circling high, a golden eagle.

You follow the moorland burn in a little green valley, an oasis in the dark peat, the banks sprinkled with the yellow and white of tormentil and bedstraw. A family of coots splashes off, round the corner you surprise a deer and a young fawn bleats at you. The burn widens into a deep still channel which merges into another lochan where you are greeted by the weird wail of a black-throated diver concerned for her single chick. Greenshanks call melodiously and flap erratically and all the while the golden plovers are piping.

Further on is a large area of marsh and reed where former leans were flooded by an old dam. Here several pairs of greylag geese are breeding; they flap up from their nests and circle, honking. More annoying is a colony of black-headed gulls which for the next mile dive-bomb and swear at you. You're glad when the raucous din finally dies away and you can soak up the peace of the remote places, ambling along a quiet shoreline as the water laps gently against the stones.

You now set off across the really rough heather and peat towards a low moorland skyline. A maze of dubh-lochs, small deep peaty pools with the bog-bean flowering in profusion, almost bars your way and you wend a tortuous route between them. From the skyline you see the distant line of the railway across the county summit and the more sinister encroaching forestry plantations which have swallowed up perhaps a third of the lower moors for slowly growing foreign pine and spruce trees.

There is still however plenty of fine moorland left and you continue for another couple of miles across the rough peat and heather. In spite of the hard going you enjoy the wide vistas, the brilliance of the day, the birdsong, the scents of wet moss and crowberry. You pick up the end of another track which runs along a small river; fish dart in the shallows and, with luck, you may see an otter playing, splashing about and trying to catch its tail.

As the evening comes on you walk down the track to the sound of drumming snipe with the curlews and lapwings calling as you reach the scrubby fields at the borders of the cultivated land. You've seen nobody all day.

Creag Scalabsdale

Do you know which is the third highest peak in Caithness? Have you ever been there?? For every ten thousand people that climb Ben Nevis, perhaps one person climbs Morven. For every thousand people who ascend Morven, maybe one visits the lonely Creag Scalabsdale, a quartzite ridge which rises to just over 1800 feet on the Sutherland Border, south of the Langwell Water and east of Kildonan.

The triangle of high ground, north of Helmsdale, almost escapes notice on a map of Scotland – but when there, you feel at the heart of the true Highlands of Scotland, the crisp hill country of John Buchan, the remote silvery horizons of Neil Gunn.

On the first truly warm day of the Spring I left the car at Berriedale and cycled past the former garden centre and on up the long track by the Langwell Water. The area around Berriedale is perhaps my favourite in Caithness with an astonishing range of cliff, woodland, moorland, valley and mountain scenery. Leaving the fine estate woodland behind, the track gave good cycling for another six miles up a magnificent little Highland glen which opened out into a broad valley below Scaraben and Morven.

Although only about 500 feet above sea-level you would think you were at least a thousand feet higher if transported here as a stranger, with Morven a fine Munro rising above. Good Grampian mountain scenery. The end of the track at Wag is however spoilt by a very ugly ruin of what must have been a shoddily built house. Piles of rubble, broken rough-casted walls, litter – it's the sort of place that unfriendly ghosts, if they exist, would haunt.

Continuing on foot, the glen opened out further round the next bend in the river, into really remote country. Brown hills, with a few patches of snow, rose enticingly into the Spring sky. The river, nicely filled with rain and the last melting snow, hurried eastwards past the remains of ancient settlements. The nearest modern habitations are probably at Braemore, six eagle miles away across Morven.

After another mile or so I climbed up through the heather to the skyline, with views opening out eastward to the sea. Steeper slopes, still cradling a large patch of snow, led up to the cairn at the eastern end of the Creag Scalabsdale ridge with an easy walk over bare stones to the top. The hills of early Spring rolled silently into the utter distance to merge with drizzle over the western coast. South, across the Cromarty, were the hills of Banff and Buchan while further west the sun shone on the snowfields of Ben Wyvis and the saddle of Carn Chuinneag with glimpses of the high Deargs. Nearer at hand the Kildonan river glinted in the sun with the railway just visible, while beyond the big lochs West of Kinbrace were the fastnesses of Ben Armine.

A horseshoe of hills – the peak I was on, Creag nan Gearr and The Child's Seat – forms a hollow holding Loch Scalabsdale, one of the sources of the Langwell Water and the highest large loch in the county. Down at its heathery shores water lapped gently in the sunshine, the larks and golden plovers were calling and all was utterly peaceful – how far, it seemed, from the anguish of the modern world.

Reluctantly I carried on, up to the top of Creag Nan Gearr, a hilltop I don't think I'd ever visited before. To my surprise, in the distance were three figures, wearing bright clothing and heading my way. Through my pocket 'spy glass' I could see that they too were looking at me, through binoculars! I waved and carried on round to the Child's Seat, a little rocky peak which is prominent from the Kildonan

Strath but is very rarely visited, other than by some large bird of prey which had left the summit rocks littered in pellets.

Large herds of deer ran off as I made my way northwards, across two miles of heather and bog to the rounded top of Cnoc an Eireannaich which forms the end of a long ridge including Morven and Scaraben. The hill must be one of the most unspectacular in Scotland but is a delectable place on a fine clear day, a high viewpoint rising out of hundreds of square miles of bog. All the lochs and pools on the Knockfin plateau were well filled and presented a spectacular sight to the north, glittering by the hundred in the sun.

Cloud was rolling in from all sides and although it was still fine and warm I could see that the north coast, including Thurso, had already disappeared into drizzle. By the time I was back at Wag the first cloud was forming on Morven – I looked at the summit through the glass and could see small flocks of birds, very high – and there, higher still, above the top, was an eagle soaring, being repeatedly mobbed by a diminuitive-looking raven.

Morven to Malvern

It's that time of year again. Only a month to go before the 'Highland Cross' with its 20-mile mountain run and 30-mile cycle; there's an urgent need for some serious training. That extra incentive to get out more and further is one of the main reasons that I, and many others, take part.

Not for me the same rabbit run, day after day. Some people even go to the lengths of running up and down flights of steps. Perhaps excusable if you lived in East Anglia but surely not in the Highlands! I do have some favourite runs, but vary them and always take any opportunity for doing something new.

The rougher the country the better, when training for the Highland Cross. A run over Morven is about as rough as they come; unfortunately I'm not fit enough to actually run up and down the peak but can at least make it to the base, WALK up and run the rest.

So – a typical Caithness Spring day, strong, raw north-west wind, cloud on the hills, showers and longer spells of rain. From Braemore a long six miles down the track to Gobernuisgeach, particularly long this time into the wind and occasional rain, and mostly uphill. Perhaps it's a bit soon to be running again after a cold… At the bothy I stop for shelter and a bite to eat, now feeling a bit better so carry on, across the footbridge and back east along the Langwell Water.

A mile on and I turn off, jogging and walking up over the rough peat and heather, aiming for the col between Morven and the white quartzite ridge of Small Mount. The ground steepens and I walk, picking my way carefully up over the piled conglomerate boulders into the mist. Soon the final, narrow ridge leads to the summit, cold tearing cloud and the odd glimpse of a view. Not a place to stop, so carry on down, a brief jog round a tongue of old snow then a slow and very careful descent over boulders and holes and heather in slippery-soled trainers. These boulders are NOT safe. One, accidentally dislodged, bounces off downwards in a cloud of sulphurous dust before disappearing out of sight with a series of thuds.

Rain drives down then clears, the slope eases off and I can run again, down grassy burns to the ancient 'Wheelhouse' by the Langwell and, more slowly, back along the track to Braemore. I'm very pleased to see that a new wooden 'kissing' gate has been put in the deer fence above the Keeper's house, with a friendly notice asking walkers to respect the stalking season and grouse moors. A much more enlightened approach than trying to keep people out with locked gates and barbed wire!

Two other hill runs could hardly have been more different. Being one of the few people in the British isles fortunate enough to have the Flow Country on my doorstep, what better than a run across it?

Very early on a rare, gloriously sunny Saturday, I drove out to Loch More, bike on the roof. The loch was flat calm, mirroring Morven, the sky deep blue, the first cuckoo calling. Caithness is rarely like this! Ten miles of pedalling took me out along the forest road, past Altnabreac, to the end of the track on Cnoc Seasaimh, a mile south of the railway. How this country has changed! Singing open moorland has been transformed into mile after identical mile of Lodgepole Pine, the road giving a fast cycle but what must be the most boring walk in the county.

From the end of the plantations the finest part of the flow country leads up onto the Heights of Knockfin. By 8.15 I was jogging west in the sunshine, past the rippling blue Lochs Eun, Mhadaidh and Rumsdale. It was very rough, and hot, yet jogging is probably the easiest way to cross the flows, the 'wavelength' of the country is just too long for walking but about right for a slow run. Down to the Rumsdale Water, follow the grassy stream banks up, up onto Channain Hill where another forest fence marks the boundary of the Hope plantations (presumably

the forester HOPES the trees will grow to produce an economic return though planted at an altitude of 1000 feet. I have little FAITH that they will)

On, up onto the high dubh-loch country of Cnoc Cromuillt before cutting down again, heading back towards the bike across five miles of peat bog, river flats and heather. The high country hill burns are delightful places on a fine day, the feeling is of utter remoteness, water cascading between grassy banks in the sun, unvisited from one year to the next. These eastern slopes of the Knockfins are one of the most special parts of Caithness.

Once back at the bike, I hammered back down the forest road towards Loch More. Although this road is well-used by locals and fishermen alike, people who don't know it mistakenly think it's exceedingly remote, and that they are the only humans for miles. On the way out I'd given a walker, heading for the station, a fright when I pedalled past at seven in the morning. Now, rounding a corner, I was greeted with the sight of a topless female walking towards me – she covered up quickly before I got close enough for a good look!

The third run was just a little different. A work trip, by plane and hired car, took me south to the English Midlands. Driving out of Birmingham airport onto a motorway packed with three lanes of high-speed traffic was certainly a shock to the system, just a few days after the solitude of the Caithness moors. Yet hills there are, and with an afternoon to spare there was still a good run to be had!

The greenery of Worcestershire was at least a month ahead of Caithness, with blossom and horse-chestnut in full flower. From the murk of Birmingham the air cleared, and little more than an hour later the car was parked at the southern end of the Malvern Hills. Remarkably for southern England, this is a ridge of ancient, Precambrian rock, rising to over 1300 feet from the flat Worcestershire plain. Very green and civilised.

The afternoon had turned fine, with puffy clouds and a fresh breeze, excellent conditions for a ten mile jog along the high spine of the hills, from one end to the other and back. The various Malvern towns roll up onto the eastern slopes of the hills, while westward stretches the hilly farmland and woods of Herefordshire, with the Welsh hills hazily seen in the distance. A long way from Morven! I some-how kept expecting to catch a glimpse of the sea to the north or east...

I'd been hoping for some refreshment in the cafe on top of the highest hill, the Worcestershire Beacon. However in the 25 years since I last saw these hills it had gone, evidently no longer considered ecologically sound. Gone too were the sheep, and the once short-cropped grass slopes were in places reverting to birch, with large patches of bluebells. Yet little else had changed. 25 years is but a clock-tick for these billion-year old hills.

The Malvern Hills. Funny where the Highland Cross takes you!

First day out

Real adventure is, for most of us, just something to read about. We can't row the Atlantic, climb the Himalayas or trek to the North Pole. We haven't the time for three months in Peru, or Tibet, we have too many responsibilities to attempt the North Wall of the Eiger.

One thing I'd love to do is another 'Hamish's Mountain Walk', a continuous walk over all the 280 or so Scottish Munros (peaks above 3000 feet). The trouble is that I can never see my way to finding the three to four months needed for the expedition. There is nothing to stop anyone, though, doing the next best thing, to go at it a week at a time..

The snag is that, by the end of a week, I am only just getting used to carrying a heavy pack over mountains and there is no way of doing as much in a day as Hamish Brown! Also I haven't the dedication, in just a short week, to slog over peaks in wild wet weather, preferring then to enjoy a walk at lower levels. But a week alone in the Scottish Highlands, walking with a pack on the back over as many peaks as weather and fitness allow, still gives a taste of the real thing.

The Kyle train was full, with a particularly loud-voiced Englishman audible throughout the carriage. I watched the scenery roll past in a dreamy sort of travel-induced daze, having set out that morning at five to walk to Georgemas Junction for the early train. It was indeed a gorgeous sunny morning, crystal clear and pleasantly cool after an early ground-frost. The late May hills still bore patches of snow, while the grassy banks near the track were thick with bluebells.

The train halted at Achnashellach and on the platform was a tall, lean, rangy figure with a pack, awaiting the east-bound train. I recognised him and as the train pulled out, shouted his name from the window, to his obvious surprise. Small world!

At just after noon I alighted at Strathcarron, climbed over the platform fence, and headed straight up into the hills without even setting foot on the road. A mile further on, I scrambled across the burn to join the 'Achintee Path', a delightful little footpath that sidles over the hills into the wilds. I say sidles. It is very curious how it keeps off skylines, skulks in hollows and little valleys, winds in and out. Perhaps it was once a smugglers trod; it certainly feels like it.

Every step, for the rest of that day, was taking me further into remote country. Once sparsely inhabited, the thousands of square miles between Strathcarron and Glen Shiel are now a true 'last great wilderness'.

The path crossed a pass at 1600 feet and descended into the grassy Bearnais glen, where Loch an Laoigh is overshadowed by the high peaks of Sheasgaich and Lurg Mhor. I cut across at the outflow and contoured round to join another path heading for Loch Calavie.

The pack, on the first day, was the heaviest of the trip, perhaps 45 pounds, but also on the first day a great sense of freedom always puts a spring in the step. Furthermore it was a perfect day of cool breeze, clear air, hot sun and dry underfoot. A day for striding miles through the hills.

The Loch Calavie path was, until recent times, an important through route; now the haunting emptiness of the remote north-west is a presence felt. Great empty peaks rise into the blue sky, water laps gently by the remains of old shielings and the sandpiper is calling, calling.

Southward, crossing the peat-bogs of Gobhlach I went, three miles west of Patt Lodge, perhaps the remotest in the Highlands and only accessible by boat up Loch Monar. A couple of miles further west is one of the finest and remotest of mountain bothies; I could see it tantalisingly in the distance but my destination lay further south, indeed as far south as I felt like walking that evening.

I turned up towards Corrie Each, rounding the corner into a vast empty glen. High peaks drew back from the spacious grassy floor and here, by the river, I put the tent up, feeling almost exposed in such a vast open landscape. 18 years before, without tent or even proper rucksac I'd come this way on my first ever big trek through the Highlands from Rannoch to Cape Wrath; this was the first time I'd been back.

I slept the sleep of the tired, like the proverbial log. Not one Munro – but a grand first day's walk!

Caithness ruins

There is a peculiar sadness about the ruined crofts and deserted farms that abound in Caithness. In southern parts such buildings have long since been renovated as holiday homes but here it is cheaper to build new, and the old crofts slowly decay.

Between Sordale and Hilliclay lie some 20 ruins and deserted crofts. The community, and all the intimate local knowledge of millennia it embodied, has totally vanished. The more recently abandoned crofts have electricity poles leading to them, and surely should never have been deserted.

Poking around such places is fascinating but demands great care in view of crumbling masonry and unsafe roofs. As you push open the mouldering door, or scramble in through the empty window frames, there is almost always a frantic fluttering as several pigeons make their escape. Mouldering furniture often remains – an old sewing machine, musty cabinets, drawers full of junk. One such used to contain a large jar of shells, whelks and groatie buckies, perhaps for the children to play with when they came to see granny. Peeling wallpaper sometimes reveals old newspaper; remote ruins often used 'Country Life' or similar with accounts of sporting activities at the turn of the century. Often the buildings have been used as a hay store or byre, and are up to the sills in straw or manure.

Older ruins are often just a gable end, broken walls with window-sills and a doorway. Somehow I never like to climb in or out over the sills, and even when entering through the doorway feel I should be knocking first. Often, in the chimney is a large metal hook for hanging the kettle above the fire, showing that this desolate ruin really was once a home. Stone shelves beside the fireplace remain, with perhaps a small shelf for the family Bible. The roofless byre still has stalls for the cows, divided by stone partitions, with square recesses in the walls for the hens to nest.

Outside, once-valuable fields are overgrown with rush and nettle, or are grazed by a few sheep. Perhaps there is a garden wall, still capped with beautifully rounded stones. There may be a remaining patch of rhubarb, or occasionally a clump of Spring daffodils or Autumn mombretia. Hidden in the rushes lie holed enamel pans, broken pottery, an old shearing tool. Very likely there will be a plough, an old stone roller, and other items of obsolete farm machinery that once were the latest innovations.

Old rusting vehicles, once somebody's pride and joy, add to the feeling of abandonment. One, near Dorrery, has a 20-year-old rowan tree growing through the remains of its engine.

Ruins or empty houses are the most poignant when in remote locations, particularly when a whole farm is abandoned and now just grazed at a low level by a few sheep or cattle. Two such lie out between the Causewaymire and Camster roads. Munsary, at the end of a three mile track from Achavanich, is in excellent shape, just silent and dead, the magnificent but hard country out of which generations carved a living now deserted. Two miles across fine dubh-loch country is the sad deserted farm of Kensary, at the end of a track leading to the Camster road. Once again a damp empty dwelling, empty byres, a mouldering threshing machine. The land is grazed by animals belonging to a farmer living miles away.

Near the road is a rotting wooden building, probably once the local school-house. This now contains an assortment of old odds and ends, including an early television set, surely a wonder when first brought home!

In spite of the fact that electricity has brought all mod cons to the remotest homes, people do not wish to live in the wilds these days. Or perhaps they seek a false materialistic standard of living which the hard life of moorland farming can never supply.

Now land is just exploited – peat is dug up, forests planted by the thousand hectares – and if we don't do something about it we may soon see skylines and hills obliterated by vast windmill arrays. Good land-use improves or works with what is already there. Meanwhile the curlews call over the empty homes, the patch by the burn where children played for 5000 years is silent. Everyone has left to join the materialistic crowds.

Cuillin heatwave

On a baking June day the main ridge of the Cuillin Hills of Skye is a desert. You can see water everywhere, the shimmering sea, the burns and rivers far below. The higher part of the ridge is however nothing but rock, black gabbro like coarse sandpaper and almost too hot to touch in places after hours of sun. Without descending 1500 feet of dusty scree and boulder into the oven of the corries, the only water available is what you've carried.

The man I met had just lost all his water and being an Australian was particularly concerned about it. He'd had the unnerving experience of watching his rucsac bounce down 500 feet of near-vertical mountainside having attempted to drop it down a little gully to make the climb easier. He'd managed to retrieve it but with bent frame, burst water bottles and dented camera. So I shared my water with him and he his mashed sandwiches with me, and for a couple of hours we encouraged each other along some tricky stretches of ridge.

Reading guide books about a place spoils a first visit. So before my first serious attempt at the Cuillin Ridge I'd read nothing and only knew a bit of the general folklore about what is sometimes called the best range of small mountains in the world. There were the Inn. Pinn. (Inaccessible Pinnacle), the Bhasteir Tooth, and the T.D. gap to contend with or bypass, somewhere on the ridge. Did one need a rope? There was never a clear answer to that question. So I went, I saw, and in three days more or less traversed the ridge, bar the odd big detour.

In fine weather, an experienced hill scrambler who is not worried by heights can get by. I'm no rock climber and have never used a rope. A bit of rock-climbing experience would however make things a lot easier. For example.

On the first day I'd gained the steeple-like summit of Sgurr Nan Gillean from Harta Corrie with no difficulty. On attempting to follow the ridge westwards I was faced with the choice of some real climbing over pinnacles with a drop of hundreds of feet on both sides, or a path which ended abruptly at a 50-foot vertical

drop with a peg in the rock from which one was supposed to abseil. After scrambling up and down false leads for half an hour I eventually found a little rock gully which was probably perfectly safe but gave a most nerve-wracking scramble to easier ground.

Climbers wax lyrical about Skye gabbro, the rough rock giving such good friction that you can't fall, the joy of climbing the friendly sun-warmed rock, the shimmering sea and distant islands around and so on. To an ordinary hill-scrambler vertical rock is impossible vertical rock and a 300-foot drop has nothing friendly about it at all. Distant views are simply not noticed as all one's concentration is on finding a safe way along and there is nothing more unnerving than finding a good path ending suddenly at the edge of a cliff.

You can, however, get round everything if you try hard enough, though you often need to make long detours down steep scree and boulder slopes, along very airy ledges with nothing on one side of them and then climb back up the scree again.

It was hot. Very hot. Even at 3000 feet. There were lots of people about and I was glad of their company; the ridge would have been just too overpowering had I had it to myself. Lots of very fit people, some doing the entire 12,000 feet of rough up and down climbing in a day (setting off at 3AM), others bivuoacing halfway along. There were fit men looking like outward bound instructors with their 12-year-old son and dog in tow, setting a pace about double mine. There was a man and wife in their 50s doing almost all of the ridge in one go.

You can even hire guides and I met one with a couple of young ladies, roped together on a stretch of ridge which even the Australian and I could walk easily. One of the peaks, Sgurr Mhic-Choinnich, gave a very fine scramble, all rock but nothing difficult or dangerous, right to the top. There was a great feeling of exposure on one bit, though you'd have had to take a running jump to fall far, and here a young lady was shuffling along the crest on her bottom, obviously not enjoying things at all. I felt just like her on other stretches.

Time passes at a different rate on fine Cuillin day. The ridge, the climbers, the steep slopes down to Loch Coruisk and that shimmering sea all round are a world detached from everything else. On two successive days I was on the ridge for more than 12 hours and meeting people who'd been out much longer.

The Inn. Pinn, the ultimate obstacle to aspiring munroists, had a queue of climbers patiently awaiting their turn. Good rock-climbers will manage it unroped, but still need to abseil off. I was content to watch them from the adjacent summit of Sgurr Dearg.

If you aren't fit you soon will be after a few days on the Cuillin. It is a near-vertical 3000-foot climb from sea-level to gain any of the peaks, then continuous strenuous up-and-down scrambling. I'd made things particularly hard for myself by keeping the tent in Harta Corrie (being too lazy to move it over to Coruisk in the heat) and so after a thigh wrenching descent of 3000 feet had then to climb back up 1200 feet of 60-degree slope to cross the intervening ridge to my tent. The compensation was an opportunity to explore several of the magnificent wild corries on the eastern side of the main ridge from a remote secluded campsite, far from the crowded sites at Sligachan and Glenbrittle.

The Cuillin hills are the closest the hillwalker can get to real mountaineering. For relaxation I can't really recommend them though. Not quite the same as the Caithness flow country (though in other respects Skye is remarkably like Caithness). The Yorkshireman I met, with teenage son in tow, summed it up nicely. Encompassing most of the main ridge in one sweep of his arm he said, 'Not quite your ordinary fell-walking country, that lot!'

June runs

Marathons and similar events are, for me at any rate, humbling experiences. It is only when running alone that the illusion (and illusion it is!) is occasionally given of being reasonably athletic.

Take one fine evening in early June. I'd left the car a couple of miles short of the Dunnet Head lighthouse and set off in the warm sunshine wearing just a running vest and shorts. Jogging west over the rough peat and heather was hard going and I was soon sweating profusely, with the sun, straight ahead, dazzling the eyes.

Half an hour later I'd reached the clifftops above the glittering sea; a carpet of blue Spring squill in the short grass. There is one geo that may be descended, with care, and I scrambled down slopes thick with yellow roseroot, pink and white thrift, red and white campion, to the shore where rollers crashed in over great boulders. Fulmars glided along the cliffs which soared red above. One feels simply unworthy amid such a scene, a trespasser into a land too good for mere humans. Such is so much of Summer Caithness and Sutherland, away from the roads.

Back on top, another 20 minutes run along the sunny clifftops led to the lighthouse where a few cars were parked and people were out admiring the sunset scenes and the cliff birdlife. It was all too easy to feel a certain sense of smugness in jogging up to the viewpoint and encountering a couple of overweight tourists with a car nearby. But who knows how far they had come, what adventures they had had – and how many locals are enterprising enough to even drive out to Dunnet Head on a fine evening? The two mile run back along the road, past the still waters of Long Loch, gave a nice ending to the run, feeling good and fit on the smooth tarmac!

As mentioned above, unless you really are one of the super fit, taking part in large events quickly dispels any illusions of athletic prowess. You meet the women

p85

who've had difficulty doing enough training, with two children aged under two. There are the sprightly veterans of 60 or 70, there are those who run 15 miles every night, there are those who have run every marathon in Scotland.

The 'Highland Cross' that year was no exception. In case you've forgotten, this annual event involves 20 miles of extremely rough hilly running from Kintail in the West through to Glen Affric and then a 30-mile bike ride down to Beauly. The organisation of this event, in which over 600 people take part, is a considerable feat in its own right. I am simply content to complete the course without finishing last, still remembering school days when I couldn't ride a bike and to run 440 yards left me in a gasping heap.

The day was fine and warm with a few cooling showers later, and as usual very wet underfoot. After all that training, as well as cycling 35 miles a day to work and back, it was a little galling not to be able to keep up with some young lady dressed in tight coloured pants with a bow in her hair! Or to be overtaken by men 15 or 20 years older than myself. I was reduced to walking before the end of the foot stage and then, on the bike, legs were cramping up while smart racing bikes went hurtling past. My chain came off and that girl whom I'd finally overtaken pedalled by and disappeared down Strath Glass.

But it was all good fun, and I finished in exactly the middle of the field in just under five hours. The winner had finished an hour and a half earlier and had probably already showered, eaten and gone home to mow his lawn. The fastest lady had beaten me by an hour. Still, 20 miles rough running and 30 miles cycling is quite an achievement in its own right, is it not? Not really. By the standards of the really fit, the Highland Cross is no more than a morning stroll.

A few years ago, somebody ran over all the peaks through which the route passes and about a dozen others as well, in under 24 hours. A distance of about 72 miles with a total ascent and descent of over 30,000 feet, more than the height of Everest, and all over the roughest of terrains. Imagine doing the Highland Cross FOUR TIMES in a row, without stopping, and you would still not have equalled that day's running. Last year I walked over about half the peaks that were climbed in the 24 hours and it took me over four days. Which all goes to show, I suppose, the folly of comparing oneself with others!

From Nevis to Dalwhinnie

Between the Winter and the midges. The last week in May and first week in June usually give the best chance of fine camping weather in the Highlands – not that snow or midges are unknown!

At 2PM, laden with a 50lb pack containing full camping gear and a week's food, I staggered off up Aonach Mor after an eight-hour journey by train, bus and the new gondola lift to 2000 feet. I had to be self-sufficient in the hills for eight days of storm or a heat, and until reaching Dalwhinnie railway station a week later would cross no roads, pass no shops.

That first day out. Always the heaviest pack, the shoulders not used to load carrying, the legs not used to mountain climbing. Slowly I slogged up the long ski-slopes into the cloud. At least I only had to climb half of the 4000-foot height of the mountain!

Once up on the plateau I needed the compass to find the way on to the higher rounded dome of Aonach Beag, still covered in old snow. All I had to do now was descend 3000 feet into Glen Nevis and camp. All I had to do. When unused to the hills, coming down steep slopes is the hardest thing, particularly with a heavy pack. The mist blew clear to reveal tremendous snow-streaked precipices all round, not a place for the careless, unless equipped with wings or a parachute. After descending 1500 feet my legs were already getting stiff; another 1000 feet down and they were shaking and aching. It was 7PM and time to stop for the night, even if a bit higher than planned. In fact I'd chosen a good spot to spend the next three nights, well up above the floor of the glen with stunning views of the Mamores and with a little waterfall nearby which provided an excellent cold shower!

The legs were so stiff the next morning that downhill walking was reduced to a hobble – so instead I went up, crossing the four Munro peaks of the Grey Corries Ridge in drifting mist and sun. Once having got up, you always get down some-how!

Munros! An arbitrary list of 280 or so Scottish peaks higher than 3000 feet. Its a sort of mountain egalitarianism. The least interesting Geal Carn rising in peat haggard slopes to 3002 feet is as much a Munro as Ben Nevis or the Inaccessible Pinnacle on Skye. And the munroist has to climb them all. 'Munro-bagging' gets a bad press, but unfairly so. This new 'sport' is actually of considerable value to the Scottish outdoor scene. Thirty years ago, when I first walked through the Highlands, you met nobody outside a few busy areas. Now, people are spread out more evenly and the Torridon peaks are almost as quiet as anywhere else. To attempt all the Munros you have to visit most of the Scottish Highlands, explore all sorts of unlikely and remote glens. You have to deal with very long walks, harsh conditions, bog and blizzard. You have to spend at least a few nights camping or in bothies. You even need a bit of rock-climbing, on Skye. Lots of magnificent peaks which nobody ever visited are now getting the attention they deserve. Munroists are not primarily to blame for erosion and litter. You need only visit some unspectacular remote peak which nobody else would climb, to see that all they have done is stamp out a faint trod, about one foot wide, where none was before. Litter is non-existent. Most of the so-called problems are dreamt up by journalists who venture no further than the local hotel bar.

The best way of getting over stiff legs is to carry on climbing. By the following evening, after 6000 feet of up and down on the spectacular Mamores ridge, they were nearly cured. On every summit I met a group of happy people, revelling in the sunshine and views, exchanging gossip about routes up and down. A lady pulled a big glossy book on the 'Great Walks' out of her rucksac – this circuit was one of them. Was the 'Devil's Ridge' OK? I was asked. Having, unknowingly, just scrambled along it I said yes, you didn't even notice it. Lancashire and London and Glasgow accents mingled on the last top in the late afternoon sun. Far below, the evening siren hooted at the Kinlochleven works.

While descending the long slopes to the glen I frightened a ptarmigan to reveal seven eggs neatly arranged around the edge of its nest. The bird stood, wings fluffed out, hissing at me from about two feet away. I carried on walking, the bird fluttering in front, pretending to have a broken wing. A hundred yards further on, a fox rose out of the heather and trotted off. It startled a deer. For a few seconds I could watch deer, fox and ptarmigan all at once.

Back at the tent, after a shower under the waterfall, I cooked tea on the Primus, watching the evening sun glowing on the peaks opposite. Rare weather indeed!

Mention hazardous mountain weather, and people think of blizzards, gales of driving rain, thunderstorms, sudden mists. However there is another weather condition which can be a force to reckon with – unbroken, scorching, sunshine. Camping in the high, bare hills gives no escape from beating sun which in June can last for nearly 18 hours of the day. It can be so overpowering that you almost start praying for rain. Many an inexperienced, unacclimatised walker has ended up in hospital with severe sunburn. It seems so foolish to be walking in hot sun with long trousers, long sleeves and a hat but when you are going to be out in the June mountain sun from 7AM till 9PM it becomes essential to spend a good part of the day covered up.

The sun shone. It shone as I walked from Glen Nevis to Loch Treig, it shone on the Loch Treig peaks, it shone early the next morning as I tramped the empty track towards Rannoch. A true Highland scene, a vast, seemingly empty land-scape, a great loch, high hills rising above snow-streaked corries, a great quiet-ness. The feeling is akin to that of walking down the nave of a great cathedral early in the morning when there are no other visitors.

Along the track towards me hurried a rambler, a smallish woman in (perhaps) her early fifties, dressed in anorak, boots and small rucsac, the sort of person whom you might expect to meet on some friendly English Lake District peak. She looked, and obviously felt, totally out of place, almost jumped when I ap-peared over a rise in the track, passed with a nervous 'hello' and hurried on. Looking back from further on I could see her skittering along the lochside path with all the mountains staring at her.

The sun shone. I'd pitched the tent at lunchtime and climbed up to a high plateau. Perhaps foolishly I'd uncovered to shorts and (definitely foolishly) left my rucsac by a prominent rock, to jog a mile or two across to visit another top. (I discovered after getting home that this was, in fact, a separate 'Munro' but didn't know it then, honest!). When nearly back I realised that there were a lot of prominent rocks, and my rucsac wasn't by the one I thought it was. By now arms and legs were burning in the sun – it was time to cover up – but clothes were in that mislaid rucsac. I rushed around for a bit and got nowhere; there was noth-ing for it but a systematic search, walking in straight lines criss-crossing the area. It took nearly half an hour to find the sack, much further over than ex-pected. Never leave your rucsac, they say.

Late next evening I was sitting at 3700 feet by the cairn of one of Scotland's remoter peaks, midway between Drumochter and Rannoch Moor. The evening sun still beat down, and the sea of distant peaks merged into the heat-haze above baking glens. Here at least the breeze was cool. My tent was pitched just 50 feet lower down, where a burn ran out of a large, rapidly melting snowfield. High camping is bold, if not foolhardy, with a 2AM rout into a rising storm always a possibility. But the weather looked calm and settled, and there were no midges!

The only snag was the sun, as on a high plateau there is no shade or shelter whatsoever.

For a couple of hours I sauntered lazily around the edge of the cliffs, watching the shadows grow in the valleys while the higher slopes turn red in the westering sun. At 10PM the sun finally dipped below the serrated peaks of Torridon, far away to the north-west and nicely framed in the entrance of the tent. The night was calm, warm and hardly dark and by 4AM it was broad daylight again. A sea of low cloud had partly spread in over the glens to the north and east but all was clear to the west, as far as the Cuillins of Skye. A few sodium lights a long way down in Roy Bridge were the only obvious sign of man. Alas, one has to sleep sometime! The hot sun on the tent roused me again a couple of hours later, to another scorching morning.

In fact the weather suddenly changed and the following evening was too cold and windy to sit for long outside the tent, pitched by a loch at a mere 2000 feet. Opportunities for comfortable high camping are rare. Yet the last day of the trip gave, surprisingly, perhaps the most perfect day of all – very clear, calm, and, again, unbroken sun. In such weather it is a joy to be out walking anywhere in the hills, and sheer torture to be imprisoned in a car.

The day's walk involved traversing the long ridge of the Fara, rising to nearly 3000 feet on the south side of Loch Ericht. A ridge of Alpine flowers, of deer cooling off in the snow patches, of an eagle soaring over the slopes below, of views up to Drumochter with those poor motorists trapped in their little beetles, glittering in the sun. The length of Loch Ericht stretched below, westward were the peaks I'd crossed in the week past.

With some time to spare I left the pack (more carefully this time!) and jogged across rough slopes for a mile to inspect the strange cleft called the Dirc Mhor. Suddenly, from smooth descending slopes, steep broken cliffs fell 500 feet to a heathery, bouldery dry valley floor, perhaps half a mile long, then rose by a simi-lar height to continue the interrupted, gentle slope down. All was still under the hot afternoon sun, just a few bees buzzing in the heather. I don't recall any birds. It felt almost as if the cleft were alive, but asleep. A strange place indeed.

By dint of clambering through new plantations and climbing a couple of deer fences I managed to reach Dalwhinnie railway station without setting foot on a road. Nothing moved in the village and the empty platform slept in the Highland sunshine. It seemed only right that the train was half an hour late (a 158 Sprinter with a sick engine), and nobody could object to sitting in the sun looking up at the hills with the deer still visible as black specks, cooling off on a distant snowfield. Eight days from Spean Bridge, 20 mountains, no roads. That night it snowed.

The best of Caithness

Caithness, as we all know, is a land of superlatives. But what would you choose as the best of Caithness? Here is my personal view!

The best town? Wick, without doubt – for character, interest, its harbour, old streets, even its cafes. The best village – Berriedale, sited in the middle of the greatest variety of countryside to be found in the county.

Think of Caithness and you think of its coastline. The coast is everywhere so magnificent that I'm tempted to say that the best stretch of coast is the one I happen to be walking along at the time! But high on the list must be the sea cliffs on the Sutherland borders, both at Drumholiston and at Ousdale. Also the cliffs between Wick and Sarclet, or Dunnet Head, or Duncansby, or … we are spoilt for choice.

Beaches? I'm not revealing my favourite, perhaps you can guess! Second best is Peedie Bay, below Dwarwick Head; for third I'm torn between Sandside and Sinclairs. Dunnet beach is fine, but can be a bit vast, and wind-blown. Fine harbours abound; I think my favourite has to be Latheronwheel, if you disallow Whaligoe!

Think of Caithness and you think of its lochs. Top of my list is Loch Tuim Ghlais, six miles walk from the nearest road and a perfect flow country loch with half a mile of sandy beach. Close in my estimation are the tiny twin binocular lochs in their hidden basins partly rimmed by crags, high on the moors South of Reay. Of the more accessible lochs, Loch More tops my list, with Calder second. The Broubster lochs, former favourites of mine, have been ruined by the forestry but many very fine flowland lochs remain…

Mountains? Morven is a clear winner but my personal favourite high hill is the remoter Creag Scalabsdale, the third highest peak in the county. Of the lower hills Beinn Nam Bad Mor, on the Shurrery estate, is my favourite, with Beinn

Ratha in second place. Of the less wild hills I think Spittal is best, for its views, with Olrig also high on the list though rather spoilt by the masts.

Stretches of river? My favourites are the Thurso at Dirlot gorge and the Dunbeath Water where it, too, runs through cliffs a few miles up from Dunbeath. Or maybe it is the Berriedale Water below Scaraben where a little suspension bridge over a deep gorge is straight out of Neil Gunn's 'Well at the World's End' – and then the Forss, near Loch Caluim, comes to mind. Spoilt for choice again.

One thing in which we are not spoilt for choice is woodland! The best is certainly Berriedale, for variety as well as stature of trees. The most interesting bit of woodland though, and indeed one of the most fascinating spots in the county, is the almost impenetrable tangle of wind-blown scots-pine mixed with birch, alder and rowan to be found on the eastern slopes of Beinn Ratha. My one hope for the new plantations is that they give rise to a bit more country like this!

Caithness animals? It is a delight to see the red deer, to hear the stags in rut, to see a fox trotting over the hill, to catch a glimpse of a wildcat crossing a road. Top of my list though would be the otter, shy and rarely seen but a most joyful animal to watch. My best sighting was on a grey December day; I was walking along a road by one of our less wild lochs when a loud whistling made me look over the bank to see an otter swimming a few yards from the shore. A second joined it, the two played at diving over each other for half a minute – before being joined by two more! For five minutes I watched the family of four otters playing in the water before they finally swam out of sight. Several cars passed meantime, you don't have go off to the back of beyond to see things in this county!

Birdlife is another great feature. The great cliff-nesting colonies of sea-birds at Duncansby, in June, are for me the best – but then there are the moorland greenshanks and golden plovers, the nonstop singing of the curlews in May, the music of the whooper swans in Winter, the cacophony of several thousand wild geese taking to the air at once, the snipe drumming on a moonlit evening in early Spring...

Which month of the year is the best? Again I'm tempted to say whichever one it happens to be at the time! Caithness weather is very rarely dull and often utterly spectacular, whether the exhilarating violence of storm-force hailstorms or 18 hours of unbroken brilliant June sun. If I had to pick a best month I think it would be June, with August (a dreadful month in most of Britain), a close competitor. If I had to sleep through a month it would be December, a very dark and stormy month full of colds and with far too much to do when one least feels like it.

What is unique to Caithness, found nowhere else? Perhaps the plateau of the Knockfin Heights, a place which may even be unique in the world. Several square miles of high peatland covered in a maze of pools and lochs of all shapes and sizes, an Arctic tundra in Winter, a naturalist's paradise in Summer. Of all the places in Caithness, I think that area tops my list of personal favourites.

Cape Wrath weekend

The early morning train rattled southwards from Kinbrace and the silence descended, almost audibly. At shortly after seven in the morning I set off pedalling down the Syre road, surely one of the emptiest in Scotland and bleak under a cold grey sky. Yet the snipe were drumming, greenshanks and golden plovers calling, and the sheep were scampering along the road in front of the bike.

June is a good time of year for long expeditions, with little darkness to worry about. My aim was to cycle out to Cape Wrath, then back home along the North coast the following day. It would be a round trip of 180 hilly miles, so I wasn't dawdling.

Ben Klibreck and the other high hills were hidden in cloud and occasional drizzle. StrathNaver was deserted, I met the first car on the twisty road along Loch Naver. The Drummore caravan site was however busy, with everyone wearing pullovers and jackets trying to keep warm. A man cutting the grass at the entrance looked as incongruous as if it had been Christmas.

On, over the Altnaharra crossroads, leaving one lonely road for a still remoter one. Drizzle and cloud still clung to the tops. Further down Strath Hope, the wind was bitter and I finally gave in and put on a woolly hat and jacket. It was colder near sea-level in June than it had been two months earlier on top of Ben Hope! Definitely not the weather for paddling but there was no boat to ferry me across the river Hope, and I wanted to take the old road to Eribol, which I'd never followed before. So I shivered knee-deep through the ford, and set off bumping along the track, looking forward to a stiff climb to warm me up,

The track was stony but rideable, except on the steeper stretches. It is shorter but much slower than cycling round by Hope Lodge. Once over the top the high peaks across Loch Eribol came into view before a hard-on-the-brakes descent of zigzags actually covered in bumpy tarmac.

Back on the 'main' road I hurtled down to the end of the loch then peched slowly back up the long miles through Laid, which always seem to give a head-

wind. Durness, everyone's idea of a tourist trap, was swarming – and depressing as usual. I went down to have a look at Smoo cave which singularly failed to impress, almost any Caithness geo is better.

A ferry takes foot passengers across the Kyle of Durness to the Cape Wrath road, from where a rickety minibus bumps for ten miles through an empty landscape to the lighthouse. It always seems to me the most unlikely of tourist attractions, I wonder how many arrive after the switchback ride feeling rather sick, to find nothing there but a cold half-gale of drizzle-laden haar.

The ferryman refused to take my bike across, presumably not needing my custom on such a busy day. To add insult to injury – 'There's no other way', said he. I didn't bother to argue. There's a perfectly good alternative route which saves the fare, it just takes an hour or two longer to detour round the end of the Kyle. I probably though shouldn't have attempted a short-cut across the sands as the tide was coming in; one of the channels was waist deep, submerging the bike and panniers. I hoped the seawater lubrication wouldn't do too much damage.

Once across, it was easy to wheel the bike along the far shore, even riding the odd hundred yards, before a hard slog up and over the hill to reach the road again. Here came the minibus, the driver waving cheerily – 'no other way' indeed. I resolved to never patronise that ferry.

The Cape Wrath road is great for bikes, utterly no traffic and nicely tarred with grass in the middle. The hills are not trivial though, the highest point is at about 600 feet but you climb at least twice that amount before you finally arrive at the lighthouse which hides itself till the last minute.

It was after six by the time I reached the end of the road, I left the bike and walked out to the north-west tip of the mainland. The weather was now bright, with a dappled sky stretching as far as Lewis in the west, Hoy in the east and Rona to the north.

Back on the bike at seven the next morning with 100 hilly miles ahead of me it felt like I'd hardly stopped moving. Up and down the road to the Kyle, back round the detour again, the channels just too deep to cross (why does the tide never seem to be favourable?). I stopped to wash the salt off the bike in a river, to the puzzled amusement of some car campers, then set off up the hills through Durness.

Apart from the fairly flat stretch through Laid, the road is one long succession of steep ups and downs all the way to Reay. But it's a most rewarding road to cycle, perhaps my favourite main road. It gets easier, honest, if you keep doing it.

Many, many hours later the gentler hills of Caithness were most welcome, even if the inevitable head-wind from the south-east had sprung up. It was slowly and stiffly that I pedalled homewards up the last long hill, just short of 12 hours after leaving the other corner of Scotland.

Beaches and bays

'A barren desert surrounded by cliffs.'? Caithness and North Sutherland folk have often disparaged the area's greatest assets – its moors and its coasts. The moors, or flow country, have belatedly attracted the world acclaim which this amazingly beautiful, diverse and species-rich landscape deserves. The coast remains mostly unknown both to locals and to the world at large.

The most conspicuous Caithness beaches, Dunnet and Keiss, would, in warmer climes, be major holiday resorts. On a bright sunny day you soon realise why few people are on the beaches, with a cold wind whipping up minor sandstorms and no shelter anywhere. The scale is also too large, somehow neither beach really lends itself to traditional seaside activities. The sea is too cold for all but the most hardy and the surfers wear wetsuits.

Yet all the way round the coast from Berriedale to Tongue there are smaller bays, rocky coves and sheltered geos where you could sunbathe all day amid magnificent scenery and have the place entirely to yourself.

Walk less than half a mile from the road and you're at a bay where seals splash and sun themselves on the rocks, where pools display a hundred different seaweeds, where there are caves, rockeries of wild flowers, a treasury of pebbles. Peace is complete – and a few hundred miles away motorways are jammed with people heading for popular resorts where the sand is dirty and the water polluted with sewage.

There is always a sheltered bay to be found, whatever the wind direction. Go to the north coast in south-east winds and when north-west winds blow go east. Get the map out, look for the little bays and explore. There are all the old herring fishing bays down the east coast, now reverted to the peace of millennia after the hectic years of the nineteenth century. There's Forse, Achastle and Sarclet to name just three; the whole coast from Dunbeath to Wick to Duncansby repays a thorough exploration.

For a small sandy bay on the east coast go to Freswick where the old Viking rubbish tip in the dunes is being eroded by wind and sea and you can see ancient limpet shells and pieces of charred bone. Duncansby is always superb; very few walk along the shell sands between the bird cliffs of the headland and John O' Groats.

Further west, visit the fine little harbours at Harrow and the Haven; pick your way across the slippery rocks to the Clett rock at Brough (but watch the tide!), look down 300 feet of steep roseroot and campion slopes to the wild rocky bay at Ashy Geo, Dunnet Head. There are the Peedie sands below the Northern Gatehouse – the best little sandy bay east of Strathy. Even Murkle Bay is nice, though often a bit smelly with rotting seaweed. Then there are Crosskirk, Brims, Sandside, the natural swimming pools at Oigins Geo…

It is however further west that the north coast really excels. The road winds inland and gives you no idea of the contorted and intricate nature of the cliffs, geos and headlands. You'll find bird cliffs, caves, puffin stacks, ancient oak ships' timbers, old headland forts (with dungeons). It would take a complete book to describe the coast in detail.

Almost any feasible rocky cove, perhaps reached by a steep scramble, was at one time used as a harbour by the desperate people cleared from the glens. Some are still in use. There are old winches, rusting rings set in the rock, perhaps a hand-line down. The only way in or out is by a narrow channel between rocks and stacks. It was truly said that the only safe port west of Scrabster was the port of eternity! You can find perhaps 20 or 30 such harbour/geos between Reay and Tongue.

For fine sandy beaches you are spoilt for choice – Melvich, Strathy, Armadale, Farr, Torrisdale, Lamigo, Port an t' Strathain, Coldbackie. The scenery and setting of all are magnificent and even on a fine Bank Holiday there is a good chance you will have the whole of a beach to yourself. The Kyle of Tongue is the distilled essence of all that is best in the Scottish Highlands.

There may be coasts in the world to equal those of Caithness and Sutherland but there can hardly be better. Why go to Spain when you can go to Strathy?

The witches of Glen Lyon

I don't believe in ghosts. Neither do I believe in witches, devils, evil spirits or other disembodied and intelligent forces of evil. There is enough real evil in the world without the need for superstition. Still, just to be on the safe side, I keep in mind the fact that, should I be wrong, the forces of good are certainly more powerful!

Consequently it is simply a series of unconnected events, perhaps even so commonplace that the term 'coincidental' is too strong to use, that I am now about to relate.

High in the remote, upper reaches of Glen Lyon in Perthshire, cut off by the Loch Lyon reservoir and under a cirque of mountains, lies Gleann Cailliche – the old woman's, or witch's, glen. Here, for thousands of years, people drove their cattle to the upland pastures for the summer and lived for a few months in the shielings. Here too lived the witch, her husband and their children, in a little stone house. They may well have been there since pre-Christian times.

The people have gone, the glen is desolate, but the witch's family remains. A set of half a dozen weirdly shaped stones, about a foot high, a bit like garden gnomes. The stones bear a remarkable resemblance to each other, each shaped like a fat dwarf with a flat hat. The largest, fattest stone is the witch's husband, the smaller stones her children. Every few hundred years (so it is said) she begats another child. The house, Tigh nam Bodach, is just big enough for the family, about a square metre in area and half a metre high, with a flat slab roof and low stone walls. Every year the local shepherd carries on an ancient custom of taking the family out of their house and arraying the figures in a row in front of it. Every Autumn they go back inside for the Winter. The witch is believed to have had enormous influence in the area in times gone by.

At the end of a very long day I was tramping in the early evening sunshine up into Glen Cailliche, full pack with camping gear on my back, feeling pretty tired.

I'd been up since 5AM, travelled by train to Pitlochry, cycled 50 miles to the end of Glen Lyon and walked six or seven miles further, all after a very busy week at work. Another mile and I'd be at Tigh Nam Bodach, where I planned to camp for two or three days.

My vision seemed a bit funny, then it developed into that familiar kink in one eye turning into a mass of pulsating, zigzagging, flashes. The beginning of a migraine – yet never before had one started when I was out in the hills. Stop, put the tent up, now! That was the clear message. I was, however, determined not to be diverted so easily from my destination and pushed on, one eye shut, stumbling over the rough heather. And, strangely, it went away, with none of the usual following symptoms of headache and sickness.

Within 20 minutes I'd reached Tigh Nam Bodach and soon had the tent pitched within sight of it, on dry grass near the river. The sun went behind the high hills, and it was six days before I saw it again.

I'm not normally one for bad dreams, but I had a strange one that night. People get them commonly I'm told, but I'd never had one like it before. I felt trapped, but couldn't move or speak, as if there was some evil power after me. I tried to say the Lord's prayer but couldn't speak – and woke up. To be on the safe side I said the prayer aloud in the tent, knowing it would put paid to any witches should such exist, and went back to sleep. I thought nothing more of it.

The next day I set off in driving rain, giving the Cailliche a friendly pat on the head in passing (with my left hand?) and managed a circuit of the Munro peaks above in decidedly poor conditions. Back in the drizzly glen that evening, a fire seemed a good idea.

Just above the tent was an area of peat littered with old pine stumps and roots; this must have been a fine stand of Scots Pine in centuries past. I pulled out various soggy bits of root and an old stump and dragged them down to the riverside. Although apparently sodden, these old roots are full of resin and, once a fire is going, burn well.

By digging out dry splinters with a penknife I soon had a fire lit. As I tried to break one long, tough root, it sprung back at me, fetching my left wrist a terrific thwack. I wriggled fingers and thumb, flexed my hand – no apparent damage done. Then, in a hurry to dig out some more dry kindling I managed to drive the penknife blade into my right thumb. It was a new knife, and very sharp, fortu-nately it hit the nail which prevented the cut being even deeper; even so it was the sort of gash that might have done with a couple of stitches. By the time I'd washed and bandaged myself up, the rain was pouring down and the fire was out.

Another circuit of hills the next day, in mist and drizzle. Back at the tent in the early afternoon, the glen was grey and gloomy, with fingers of mist reaching ever lower. Another night there didn't appeal, it was time to move on. It was not that easy, though. My left wrist had become increasingly sore and swollen, and made nasty creaking noises whenever I bent it. In the end I had to bandage and splint it. That, combined with my damaged thumb, made the cycling and camping for the rest of that week a little more difficult than usual.

I spent two more days in Glen Lyon but the weather never relented and it wasn't till I left the glen altogether that the sun came out.

The migraine, the bad dream, the damaged wrist, the cut thumb – just little things that could happen to any hill camper.

Poor witch! All the people who knew, and respected her, gone for centuries. All her influence gone. All she gets now is the odd interloper who camps on her doorstep, makes a fire from the remains of her favourite trees and doesn't be-lieve she's any more than a strangely shaped stone. You can't help but feel sorry for the neglected Cailliche and her family.

Helmsdale to
Cape Wrath

The afternoon's steady rain had cleared, but evening showers still swept in on a blustery west wind. Shafts of sun between dark clouds gleamed on loch and wet rock slab below misty summits. On the very summit of Ben Stumanadh, as cold rain swept across again, a mother ptarmigan fluttered off from my feet while her chicks, tiny balls of fluff, scattered. The handsome chestnut and white bird shuffled along just out of reach in front of me, pretending a broken wing, I chased after her so that once well away from her chicks she'd take off and circle back to give them shelter from the wet cold. Somehow she had successfully hatched her brood after sitting on her eggs on that exposed summit throughout a long cold May. Hardy birds!

As the cloud and rain cleared again I jogged back down the steep hillside to birchwoods where a cuckoo called incessantly. Third night out, nearly half way.

For once I hadn't quite felt like spending a week in the hills dragging a bike over the Grampians or frantically bagging Munros in the wet West. Instead I'd decided to take things easy and spend the week wandering along a chain of bothies from Helmsdale to Cape Wrath, across the wild and peaceful heart of Caithness and Sutherland. By aiming to restock food in Tongue there was never a need to carry more than four days' supply of food and without a tent the load could be kept to fairly comfortable levels.

How nice to be catching the early train from Georgemas Junction only as far as Helmsdale! The last time I'd set off on that train it had been for a round trip of 1600 miles. Nice too to start walking sensibly early on the first day, out along the Kildonan road before eight. Indeed those two miles of road, with a further seven or eight through Tongue, were almost all of about 130 miles which weren't across rough, pathless country. Who needs long distance paths? The 1:50,000 maps are far better than any guide book and countless possibilities for cross-country walks leap out at you – all you need is the time to walk them!

There is a grand sense of freedom on these treks, even if weighed down by a pack and susceptible to vagaries of weather. No deadlines, no need to rush, lots of time just to think, and watch, and listen. Great to turn off the road into the hills knowing that you don't have to return to a car, that there are no more roads for three days! Slowly I climbed the heathery slopes of Cnoc na Maoile, new country for me although so near home. Deer were low down for early June and Spring was only just coming to the higher slopes with a cold wind blowing over the great expanses of yellow and brown moor. Five miles ahead, across the headwaters of the Langwell Water, was the col I was making for between Morven and the neighbouring Small Mount.

Now, and for the following two days, I was crossing the great flow country, the largest area of peatland in the world. I sloshed, plowtered and squelched over, through and round every variety of peatbog and moor known to man. Yet there was nothing dismal or depressing about it, indeed quite the opposite. The vast expanses of open moor, the skyscapes, the birds, the deer, the sun and the constant wind, are inspiring, it's mostly a landscape that would look much the same if man had never settled in Scotland. In the third Millennium in overcrowded Britain it is still possible to walk for miles and miles without crossing roads, paths, fences or even drainage ditches, without seeing masts, or pylons, without hearing planes or cars. In a whole week I met nobody at the bothies or on the moors and mountains. Not even footprints in the peat. Where else can you do that these days?

With all the time in the world I detoured from the col up to the top of Morven, even though I'd only been there a few weeks before. It's a sin to have got into the habit of doing things in such a RUSH, to drive out to Braemor, run over Morven or Scaraben and be home for lunch, or to run round Dunnet Head in a morning. These places need time to appreciate them properly and now I was making some amends.

Another couple of miles took me to the bothy where I'd be spending my first night. To mention the locations of bothies in print is these days regarded as a heinous crime and to avoid being flung out of the Mountain Bothies Association I'll have to be circumspect. Vandalism and over-use can be serious problems but anyone really keen on the outdoors will in any case have little difficulty in finding the locations of these havens.

An hour or two of sitting out reading, pottering around collecting wood, cooking over a fire, an evening walk along the river or up the local hill and a really good night's sleep – that's a bothy night. No tent to put up or take down, ample time to collect wood for others, to sweep the place out, leave it welcoming for the next visitor – and to make sure the door is properly closed and fastened! Bothies full of dead sheep are not nice.

The second day was to be a long one, there was no option without a tent. Right across the Knockfin Heights, down to Achentoul, up over Ben Griam Beg and then across knobbly loch and very wet bog country to the upper reaches of the River Strathy. Only the start of the day was dry underfoot, following the river and then the hill burns right up onto the Knockfin plateau. I love these quiet and remote high Caithness glens, virtually untrodden by modern man. You round a corner and there's a party of hinds feeding, or a family of ducklings on a slack pool.

Some care is needed on the Knockfin plateau, it's very wet and quite a maze of bog and dubh-loch. At one point I found myself knee-deep in black ooze where I'd tried a dubious short-cut. If in any doubt about the bog, go round! A mile in the Highlands may be worth two elsewhere, but a mile in pathless Sutherland is worth more like three. It is not uncommon in particularly rough going to be making barely one mile per hour.

A trig point marks the summit of the Knockfins, a good place to be on one of those glorious clear days of blue sky and cumulus with the moors stretching for ever in all directions. The top of Ben Griam Beg, my next destination, was still three hours walk away, down, across an area of rough bogs to the road, then along the easy Griamachary track for a couple of miles. Griam Beg is another hill that's usually rushed and it was good to have ample time to appreciate the views over miles of lochan and moor. Far in the distance I could just make out the roof of my next bothy, another three hours walk away, rounding Loch Crocach to descend from Cnoc nam Tri Chlach (Hill of the three stones – prominent landmarks from the east) to near the remote Loch Strathy. Those last miles were long, never was a brew-up of tea at the bothy more appreciated!

When you have to go home after a day out you miss the best part of the day, the long evenings in the high moor and hill country, the late sun, the evening scents and birdsong, the complete peace. Perhaps the sense of remoteness is a bit artificial, people lived in these bothies, after all, till at least the nineteen-forties, and usually raised large families. Central Sutherland has however always been mostly empty, only the fertile straths were once populated.

Monday morning, instead of going to work I was heading west in glorious sunshine, across remotest Sutherland by the sandy shores of Loch Strathy. Cloud was spilling in fast though and a rising south wind promised rain later. The landscape was now hillier and by keeping to the hillsides and avoiding the large flow areas I managed to keep my feet dry for the rest of the crossing to StrathNaver. The valley opened out below from above Rhifail, very lush and green compared with the surrounding moorland. Straight down, across the bridge, and up the other side and in an hour or so back into the familiar peat-bog and tussock landscape.

The route westward towards Ben Stumanadh crossed some very rough wet flows on the approaches to the increasingly rugged hills to the south of Borgie Forest. The promised rain had arrived on a cold, rising gale so I took a contouring route, passing through recently fenced old birch woods. Already a thicket of young birch and rowan was growing up with the protection afforded from browsing deer. It was good to reach the bothy by mid-afternoon, to collect wood and sit by the fire with a hot cup of tea. Stumanadh would be climbed that evening then on tomorrow by Tongue towards Whiten Head. The one deadline I had was to be at Kinlochbervie by nine on Saturday morning for the Post Bus to Lairg, otherwise the freedom of the far north was mine!

The following morning was fresh and blustery, with spectacular views across the Kyle to Ben Loyal and Ben Hope and it was exhilarating, after three pathless days, to stride the easy miles along the main Lairg-Tongue road. The Tongue Post Office shop was a marvellous place after several strenuous days on camping rations, with mouth-watering delicacies like real bread, pork-pies, cheese and yoghourts in bewildering quantity. Nothing like fresh air and exercise to make you appreciate real food! Half an hour later, laden with my next four days' supplies and with a good few hundred calories already consumed, I was on my way again.

Anyone who comes this way should cross the Tongue Causeway on foot from time to time, it's one of the best places to appreciate the finest scenery in Scotland, especially on a clear, breezy day with white wavetops on the Kyle and spray blowing across the road. Terns and oyster-catchers screeched at me. Another couple of miles led up the Moin road before turning off to the right, into pathless moor again, for the miles across to Whiten head.

The Moin is one of the most spectacular, or the most dismal, features in Sutherland, depending on your viewpoint. Perhaps 30 square miles of pathless peatbog, an ornithologist's or botanist's dream, crossed by one road, rising to an altitude of around 800 feet between Loch Eribol and the Kyle of Tongue. To cross on foot is an experience, mile after mile of squelching through and around bog and diver-haunted dubh loch. On a clear day the tremendous views and sense of space give an impression that you are alone on the planet; in mist and wild weather and approaching darkness you really feel that you are. Fifteen years ago, almost the whole area was burnt in huge fires, the vegetation is still slowly recovering. The new road, constructed ten years ago, was dug straight through dubh-lochs and peat which had accumulated for 8000 years. Yet much of the area is still reasonably pristine, let us hope that the value of such a place is now recognised and it can be preserved from forestry or wind farms or quarrying or other destructive 'developments'!

So, down to the rocky shores of Eribol, a driftwood fire in the bothy that night, then back south along the shore-line in rising wind the next morning. From Hope

Lodge the easy route would follow the main road, instead I chose to follow the rough watershed over various knobbly hills above Loch Hope. After some vicious squalls of rain the weather cleared a little but the wind was still rising, and progress over the rough country became slower and slower. Sheets of spray were being whipped off the lochans, indicating at least force nine. On the 1700-foot top of An Lean-charn it was difficult to stand, with a fight into the wind to get down to the west. This was June!

Now I headed into the wildest and roughest part of Sutherland below Foinaven, an area where if the ground isn't peat-bog it's rock slab at all angles from horizontal to vertical, or boulder scree, or loch. Some old birch woods cling to near-vertical slopes and are now, at long last, being fenced to allow regeneration. One can but admire the skill of the fencing contractor in placing deer fences up 60 degree slopes of boulder and crag overgrown with trees. The combination and variety of habitats here – sea-shore, peat-bog and dubh loch, sheltered woodland, crag, moor, mountain-top, even some forestry and farm-land – is astonishing. Fortunately the Eribol super-quarry proposal has been shelved.

The wind funnelling down the strath must have been at least force ten in the night but had moderated (a good thing too) by the morning of what was going to be a long day, across Cranstackie and Farrmheall into the Parph country south of Cape Wrath. One hears of 'lunar landscapes' but on the slopes of Cranstackie this is no exaggeration. The south 'ridge' comprises miles of gently-sloping bare rock and boulder, with almost no vegetation at all. The western slopes, once away from the summit, were however surprisingly green and the farm of Rhigolter, down in the valley to the south of the Kyle of Durness, basked in the June sun. It would not have seemed so idyllic the night before!

A good track took me to the road and one of the delights of this sort of walk, to step on tarmac just to cross from one side to the other before setting off into the wilds once more. I feel really sorry for car and caravan tourists, isolated from the environment and imprisoned in or near their vehicles, seemingly taking everything with them instead of getting away from it all,

Once again the country had changed. Now I was entering the Parph, a hundred square miles of grass and rush-covered boggy moorland, high rounded hills with lonely wind-scoured stony summits, a few steep crags and a rugged coastline. Hoy is similar, but on a smaller scale. Having already crossed Cranstackie there were still hours of walking ahead, first a long slow climb to the 1700-foot top of Farrmheall above the Gualin House, then a steep descent and miles down the bogs of Strath Shinary towards Sandwood Bay. No hurry though, no deadlines. Tired? just sit down for ten minutes by the green grass of a spring on the side of Farrmheall, admire the sun glittering on the flows around Feur

Loch, listen to the golden plovers calling, It's easy to fall into the trap on these trips of just battering on to reach one's destination instead of taking the time to appreciate what one may never have the opportunity to do again.

It had turned really warm, indeed warm enough for a swim in a river pool, after which the last mile to the bothy didn't seem so long.

On the last full day I was committed to a walk of at least 20 miles in order to reach Cape Wrath and return to the bothy for a second night. The weather was ideal, dry, clear, warm but with a cool sea-breeze on the cliff-tops. First some six pathless miles to the cliffs at the Bay of Keisgaig, passing a bothy where a hermit used to live, giving rise to stories about Sandwood Bay being haunted.

At Keisgaig, as planned, I changed from boots into old trainers and left the rucksac, to jog as much as possible of the remaining four miles to the Cape Wrath lighthouse. Not an easy jog; rough with much up and down, but magnificent scenery and views all round, as always on a fine day on the clifftops. This remote spot with its lighthouse (manned until 1998) is an unlikely tourist attraction, yet mini-buses shuttle to and fro along the bumpy road which twists for ten miles from the Durness Ferry.

I jogged round the back of the lighthouse, in scenery very like Strathy Point or Duncansby Head, then across to the road, surprising a crowd alighting from one of the buses. An hour later I was back at the Bay of Keisgaig for a celebratory lunch.

My main objective achieved, there was now plenty of time to enjoy the glorious weather by pottering along the cliffs to Sandwood Bay. This used to be a bit of a nudist and hippy place, cars could be driven along the rough road to within half-a mile of the sands. Now owned by the John Muir trust, all has changed, you have to walk at least four miles to get there and the bay is again as magnificent as its reputation. It's a bit like the northern end of Aird Torrisdale and Invernaver where sand has drifted up the rocky slopes; Mountain Avens and Cushion Pink saxifrage were in full bloom. The main bay is a sweep of sand like Dunnet, but with a large freshwater loch just behind the sand-dunes. Two people I met – almost the only two on the whole trip – reckoned that on such a day it must be one of the most beautiful places in the world.

It was certainly a place to linger but there was a long, rough walk yet back to the bothy, a place I was very glad to reach after a struggle along the wrong side of the loch. All that remained then was an early start the next day, five miles walk across the knobbly hills to Kinlochbervie, and a long ride home by Post-Bus to Lairg and train back to Thurso. Seven leisurely days walking across the incomparable Caithness and Sutherland landscape, seven bothy nights – and barely one other walker. Not all of this world has yet been spoilt.

Coast-to-coast madness

West coast weather. All too familiar to anyone who has lived or travelled in the mountains of Western Britain, from Snowdonia to Sutherland. A screaming Atlantic depression, westerly winds sweeping sheets of rain across cloud-enveloped hills. White water cascading in long ribbons down the hillsides, rivers in full spate. Water everywhere that ever sees water. Highland Cross Day.

Every year I take part in this crazy mid-summer biathlon from Kintail on the west coast to Beauly on the east, 20 miles running over mountain paths and tracks, then 30 road miles on the bike. Only the fact that the event raises huge sums of money for charity justifies the sheer insanity of it. In 1995 – well, you could only laugh, hysterically.

A fleet of buses takes 600 competitors from Beauly and Inverness across to the start in Glen Shiel, a fleet of lorries transports the bicycles to the end of Glen Affric. The event is organised like a military campaign.

Light rain all night in the Beauly area was a warning of things to come. As always, though, the bus was a hubbub of enthusiastic conversation as we ground over the long hills to Drumnadrochit – or droochit, that morning. By the time we reached Glen Shiel the real conditions were becoming apparent. It had obviously been raining for a long time, and didn't look like stopping. Rain hosed the bus, the odd drop finding its way inside through the top front windows. A few swerves to avoid minor floods caused some excitement on the top deck. At the sight of the swollen waterfalls pouring off the Five Sisters, conversation became a bit more muted and people began to realise what they might be in for.

Many must have been tempted to stay on the bus and ride back to Inverness, rather than alight into the cold driving rain at Morvich. But we were committed now; there were 20 miles of rain-soaked glens to traverse to reach the waiting bikes at the end of Glen Affric. Everyone was strangely quiet walking along the short stretch of road to the start. People were huddling under trees, by buildings, keeping warmer clothes on as long as possible. 600 shivering and rain-swept runners waited for the start, delayed ten minutes by some who had been on a late bus. You could only laugh. What were we doing here!

At last the start… just 200 yards into the run and the track vanished under a foot of water. Like sheep forced through a sheep-dip everyone in the still tightly-packed cavalcade of runners had to splash straight through the middle. 'Well, that's my new trainers properly christened' commented somebody. We were all going to get a pretty good baptism by the end of the day.

Conditions were the worst ever in the Highland Cross. Every few hundred yards were swollen streams, knee deep at least, to splash through. Often the path was a river, or hidden under black peaty pools, churned up by previous runners. Into these you plunged, hoping for the best. Everyone was in up to their waist at some time or other. People were slipping and sliding on wet grass and peat, stumbling and sitting down in the middle of rivers, plunging in thigh deep where they'd expected to go in up to the ankle.

Some compensation was the sight of the Glen Lichd falls, most spectacular in full spate and with a long line of brightly clad runners wending their way along the steep narrow path, high above. Fortunately the wind was from behind as the rain was cold and stinging when, briefly, the path turned towards it.

At the crest of the path a man was standing, relaying radio messages. Wrapped in yellow oilskins and many layers of clothing he looked as impervious to the weather as a rock. As I passed, I caught the tail end of his message, '…can confirm that the back-marker is English'. I'm still wondering what the significance of that could have been. Perhaps they reckoned that only weather-toughened Highlanders were up to the conditions!

The descent towards the Affric Hostel was a hilarious mixture of water-slide and battlefield trenches, of split-second choices between risking bottomless black peat or bottomless green moss. The main river was too high to ford and we were diverted over a rickety footbridge, reached by running over pathless peathags where I felt quite at home!

The path from then on gradually improved, with only a few more deep rivers to cross. The rain, too was dying out. But the effort of running 14 miles in such conditions showed by the time we reached the dreaded last six miles of forestry track – the yellow brick road.

Normally by now my muscles and feet would be complaining; surprisingly these were OK. I just felt really tired. After all the twisting and jarring of the cross country this hilly forestry road is a real killer. Even in good conditions all but the fittest are forced into walking the steeper sections. The scenery, Loch Affric, the ancient Scots pines, the mountains, do little to take the mind off the pain. Those six miles were no fun, the final mile, on tarmac, the worst. At last the changeover point, lots of bikes still there so I wasn't doing too badly.

The delight at reaching the bikes is only surpassed by that of actually finishing. I sat down (would I manage to get up again!) to change into dry socks and shoes, put T-shirt and helmet on, munch a biscuit. If I could manage the first few miles on the bike I'd make it. Once again, the superb scenery of Glen Affric was hardly seen in the push to reach Beauly as quickly as possible. The road is closed to traffic, the cycling can be exhilarating. Hurtling down the steep bends to Cannich is the closest an ordinary mortal will come to descending the Alps on the Tour de France. An ambulance is usually parked on the steepest section, door open, waiting for the almost inevitable casualties…

This time however even the cycling was hard, my energy had mostly gone. Instead of overtaking many I just passed a few and a few passed me. There was no exhilaration to it, just a hard grind for the 30 miles down Glen Affric and Strath Glass. The finish was great though, a carnival atmosphere, pipe band playing, hundreds of people. As usual, I could hardly walk. It had taken me just over five hours, which was ten minutes slower than the previous year.

One of the best things about the Highland Cross is the buffet meal laid on by the Beauly churches and WI – soup, tea and a nice light salad. Great to sit sipping hot sweet tea, looking at all the other haggard but happy faces and hearing of the adventures of others along the way! Everyone had found it hard, and even the winning time was over 15 minutes down on last year's. So in the end I finished further up the field then usual. 'Horrendous' was a word that cropped up frequently in conversation. Yet everyone seemed keen to run again the following year. Why? You may well ask!

Mountain biking

I don't suppose there are many who have ridden a bike laden with full camping gear along a 3000-foot high Scottish mountain ridge, wearing only helmet and boots, before eight in the morning. The idea of doing five impossible things before breakfast has always appealed to me …

Most hill days follow a standard pattern, a start in the morning from the valley or the town, a day spent on the tops then an evening back in the valley again. This day was the complete opposite, beginning and ending at over 3000 feet with a descent to the town around lunchtime.

South of Braemar and Balmoral lies a huge rolling plateau, over 50 square miles in extent and much of it above the 3000-foot contour. For three days I'd explored the high tops, from Lochnagar in the east to the Glenshee hills in the west and the peaks above Glen Clova to the south. Three long days days of sun and broken cloud, striding out across vast bare grassy slopes above deep valleys, the only company mountain hares and ptarmigan.

The day before had begun with a double-pack up 2000 feet of 30 degree slopes – first climbing up to the ridge with the bike from Glen Callater then going down again for the pack. The air was calm and even at 3000 feet it was already hot, it would be baking in the glens. I'd put the tent up on the plateau and spent the rest of the day jogging out to the outlying munro tops of Mayer and Dreish.

Now on my way again, I aimed to cross the 3250-foot top of Broad Cairn and pick up a track down to Loch Muick. The path from Cairn Bannoch to Broad Cairn was smooth and easy to cycle – until the boulder fields. Try climbing over piled rocks with a heavily-laden bike! Eventually, after much strenuous activity, I reached the summit with hopes of a slightly easier descent ahead.

A few years ago it was fashionable for estates to bulldoze Land-Rover tracks high into the mountains giving lazy guests easy access to the deer and grouse. Rapid erosion has now turned many into river beds, scars on the landscape and of no use to vehicle, pedestrian or cyclist. One such ends only 500 feet below the summit of Broad Cairn, the bike had to be slowly wheeled down it, bumping over loose fist-sized, and bigger, rocks.

The track gradually improved till I could ride, high up with increasingly spectacular views across Loch Muick, over 1000 feet below. Then it plunged downwards in steep 1 in 3 zigzags. I tried to ride but the load on the bike was too great, the back wheel slipped sideways and all the weight nearly came on top of me. Walking was only a bit easier. Grampian granite erodes to small gravel which behaves like ball-bearings to a heavy bike trying to slide off a mountain. I survived. Once down by the loch I surprised a couple who'd met me three days earlier on the other side of Lochnagar –

' How did you get here?'

Difficulties over, it was an easy ride down the track to the Glen Muick car-park, well-filled with crowds heading for Lochnagar. The rest of the glen gave a coast down to Ballater, the trees and rocky river a pleasant contrast to the bare hills I'd been in for the previous three days.

The town was bustling and hot, but I needed supplies. My next destination, Mount Keen, could be reached by an adventurous route over the hills or an easier, but longer, route by roads and tracks. In the heat I didn't fancy another struggle with bike and pack across the mountains and took the coward's route, down the easy road south of the Dee towards Aboyne.

In spite of the lush woods, the greenery, the birdsong, the river, I was already hankering after the high hills and glad at last to turn off onto a rough track, the old Mounth Road across to Glen Tanar. The start was delightful, along a Grampian lane of rounded boulder walls and wild flowers, even if the hill was too steep to ride. Better still was a long gentle descent around the side of Glen Tanar, nicely by-passing the huge visitor centre at the foot of the glen.

Indeed, Glen Tanar is very fine with the river and the native Scots Pine woods, only the steady climb into a fresh head-wind under the hot sun detracted. Ants scurried to and fro across the track, a sure sign of a genuine old forest. Further on I cycled round an adder, stretched out in the sun – it suddenly coiled up like a spring then shot off the track – they can move fast!

At the head of the glen, below Mount Keen, there used to be a very fine bothy. The story goes that a party staying there left a fire burning and went off to climb Mount Keen in the evening, coming back to find a rather larger fire than they'd intended. The house was completely destroyed, only piled stones now remain. I'd thought of camping nearby but the glen was rather open and it was a bit too much like a camp-site, obviously much used by others. The weather looked settled. I'd camp a little higher.

Two hours later and the tent was pitched on the very summit of Mount Keen. I've visited all but about 50 Munro summits but my real ambition is to camp on top of them all (Having only managed about four so far, its an ambition that's very unlikely ever to be realised). It's great to spend hours on a summit instead of the usual cursory ten-minute visit. Mount Keen might seem a bleak, bare top but all kinds of life emerges after a while. A young mountain hare. Ptarmigan, croaking and running nearby. Grouse calling lower down. A lark hopping around the summit rocks.

Glens and rolling ridges receded into distant heat-haze, a huge area of country to the south and east in which I'd never set foot. Later in the evening mist rolled in from the sea (30 miles away), strangely keeping just to the east of the top with the low sun throwing my shadow onto it as the famous 'Brocken Spectre'. Very late, a few distant lights gleamed from farms and houses, far below. Very early, the dawn sun warmed the tent. To wake up, already on top of a high mountain – that's a good way to start a day and one impossible thing already done before breakfast!

The remotest bothies

It was nearly midnight and the gloaming was turning into a deep mountain dusk at the end of a long July day as I splashed through the last river and picked my way round the bogs to the bothy.

I'd left home before six that Saturday morning, cycled down to Georgemas and sat on the train to Muir of Ord. The train was full of bikes and I met somebody else planning, like me, to cycle up Strathfarrar. We got talking about things that go wrong with bikes and having taken my old machine (repaired with glue) I was getting serious misgivings as to whether it would last more than a few miles. My mind was made up however to visit two remote bothies in the country north-

west of Glen Affric, even if it meant a long walk through the night! Fortunately the bike held together.

The day was fine and mild, but with a stiff head wind. I took the leafy lanes south of the River Beauly, by Keskadale, emerging at Struy opposite the entrance to Strathfarrar. This superb glen, 20 miles long, is little known other than by hillwalkers. You can drive a car up, obtaining a permit at a locked gate; there are native pinewoods as good as the better known woods of Glen Affric and there is some grand mountain scenery at the head of the glen, even if it's a bit spoilt by man's hydroelectric activities. The little road twisting through woods, by river and loch, is however really designed for cyclists who need no permit to travel this way.

By early afternoon I'd ridden the bike to the end of the road and set off on foot up the path leading westward below the slopes of An Riabhachan. It was another ten miles over the hills to the bothy, about half of the distance on paths and the rest over typical rough peat and heather, with a couple of passes to cross. The afternoon was cool and cloudy but dry with the wind keeping insects away. Although today all this country is very remote, people used to live here and there are many paths. The grassy slopes of An Riabhachan are streaked with old drainage ditches, cut to improve the Summer pastures at altitudes of up to 2500 feet.

At the bothy I quickly ate a tin of meat and some biscuits and cake, with tea brewed on a fire of dead heather, before setting off again at 6.30 PM to visit a neighbouring bothy, some six rough miles away. It would be a rush to get back before dark.

My route led diagonally across the side of the peak to the north; the slopes were alive with deer, some with young. A short-cut along the pathless west shore of dark loch Calavie proved very rough and saved no time and it was good to rejoin the path again; in such rough country a path is twice as fast and half the effort. But all too soon I had climb up over the slopes of Lurg Mhor to get round into the next glen – and there was the loch with the bothy still a speck a long two miles away. The scenery here is truly spectacular with steep peaks all round – also this is one of the wettest spots in the north-west and already drizzly showers were creeping in.

There were people across the loch, fishing, and smoke was coming from the bothy chimney. Nobody was in when I got there but hillwalking gear, food and sleeping bags were strewn everywhere with on the table a pile of cans of beer and bottles of vodka that could have served a small bar. I didn't linger, and headed straight back the way I'd come, no doubt to the concern of the party by the loch who had seen this lone figure coming down from the hills to the bothy, looking inside, then disappearing back the way he had come into the late evening cloud and drizzle …

From London to Reay

A grey squirrel ran along the ground and others chattered in the trees, it was bright, and as nice an early morning as you could hope to get in the soulless heart of the stockbroker belt, south-east of London. I jogged along an avenue where huge mansion houses overlooked a few fields and trees, where a small flat would cost over half a million. Some of us would pay a sum like that to live as far away as possible.

London was sticky and hot, the tube out to Heathrow was sweaty and packed. The best thing about this part of the journey was discovering that I could get a free cold shower at the airport! The plane climbed out of the pool of murk which almost always overlies the south, then up through cloud which hid the views till we started descending through frontal cirrus at 28,000 feet over the Cairngorms. There was a brief glimpse of Aviemore and the A9 before landing ten minutes later at Inverness. In the clear air you could see the mountains 40 miles away, it was warm but not that humid stale air of London.

Just ten minutes walk from the airport and I was in a Scots Pine wood, among heather and wild raspberries, with a spare hour to work the city out of my system before catching the little eight-seater plane up to Wick.

So just a few hours after leaving London suburbia I was jogging over the Hill of Olrig, feeling like an escaped prisoner running free across the top of the world. In the clear northern light of Caithness it was very hard to understand why so many people inflict such a miserable existence on themselves in south-east England!

Early the following morning saw me striding out down the track south of Reay towards Beinn Ratha under grey skies which threatened to add more rain to an already substantial overnight total. Several windblown plantations of pine straggle the eastern slopes of Ratha, fascinating places and havens of wildlife. I scrambled around in one of them amid a tangle of fallen pine, young birch, rowan, bramble and bog – with a few decent trees still more or less upright. There may be a lot of country like this in Caithness in 50 years time! Woodland birds sang and fluttered in the trees, red deer hinds splashed off through knee-deep bog.

Fighting my way out of the thickets I climbed up above the banks of a stream which roared over little waterfalls from its source in bogs below a moorland crest. For a couple of miles I splashed through sphagnum and heather along the watershed, still revelling in the freedom of the uncluttered empty open spaces. In the south, on a cloudy day, you can never see more than a few miles – here all horizons were sharp except where Ben Loyal was disappearing into a haze of approaching rain.

The deep little valley of the upper reaches of Sandside Burn fell away below me; I scrambled down, passing sites where eagles once nested but, alas, have long since left. This is a grand little glen to follow all the way back to Reay, real Highland country, so near and so little known.

The weather cleared over lunch and we all went down to Peedie Bay for the afternoon. The sun was warm, the air was clear, we just enjoyed the sea, rock and cliff scenery. As we set off up the hill to be home for tea the wind was rising again, with the first blustery showers moving in from the west.

The occasional trip south does one good. You realise how few people in Britain are fortunate enough to be able to spend a morning in the wild open spaces of moor and mountain and an afternoon in the sun on a quiet, clean sandy beach amid superb scenery. There may be better places in the world to live, but they are few.

Shenavall

Shenavall must be, after Corrour in the Cairngorms, the best known bothy in Scotland. Indeed it's so well known that I need have no worries about mentioning its location in print. Shenavall lies just ten miles south of Ullapool, an easy, if boggy, four-mile walk over the hill from the Gairloch road.

It's the friendliest of places – a rambling house of six or seven rooms, a couple of fireplaces, the usual bothy assortment of furniture rescued from tips and old cars, and reputedly a ghost. The situation is superb with the tiers of sandstone crags of An Teallach (The Forge) rising for 3000 feet at the back while a wide expanse of deer-grazed grass and rush leads down to the loch. Beyond rises Ben Dearg Mhor, like a huge armchair, with a great crater of a corrie below crags that look a mile high.

Southward stretches some very remote country, a tangle of rugged mountain and loch, an area well-known to connoisseurs of the wild places. Indeed the area has become so busy in recent years that it's advisable to take a tent in case the bothy is packed out.

Everyone who visits Shenavall takes away fond memories. My first visit was in the mid-seventies. For three weeks I'd been trekking north from Rannoch through bog, storm and flood. It had rained for at least several hours every day. The day had looked like another repeat, thickening high cloud and rising wind, but this time things were different. As I tramped through the glens from Loch Fannich, the clouds started to retreat again. Great slabs of wet rock, high above, began to gleam in the sun.

At the end of a long day, Shenavall came into sight, the sun glowing on the warm sandstone of An Teallach. Smoke was coming from the chimney and in residence were two American girls, with tea brewing on the fire as I walked in the door. (Ask any red-blooded male bothy-goer and the dream is always of the woman that might be at the next bothy. Once in a lifetime it happens. In 1974 I'd just arrived at the Galloway bothy of Backhill of Bush, during a heatwave, when an attractive and unaccompanied young lady walked in the door wearing almost nothing. 'Excuse me', she said, 'But I've just bathed!')

The next day, the first truly fine day for three weeks, I wandered the high ridges of An Teallach, revelling in the sun and the views, and at five the following morning climbed Ben Dearg Mhor before returning to the bothy for a second bowl of porridge and a walk out to Ullapool.

A few years later and another trek, north to Cape Wrath, again not the best of weather. I'd decided to sit out a downpour by Loch Fada, hoping for an improvement in the afternoon. None came; instead I had to pack and move the tent out of reach of a rising burn. It was the sort of day from which the camper prays for deliverance.

The next day gave similar weather but driven by frustration I managed to lug tent and gear across three craggy, bouldery peaks (later to be upgraded to 'Munro' status) in mist and rain. My old map was badly wrong, marking a triple peak as a plateau and totally ignoring high crags which barred the way as I descended through mist towards the bothy. I had to go back up and cast around for a different route, eventually managing a slow, rough descent of 3000 feet to the swollen river – already soaked, I just waded through with all my clothes on.

The bothy was a haven that night. An Teallach was forging the showers which lashed down, one after another, and it was great to be under a roof after nights of camping in rain-swept, sodden glens. (After another week of tramping and camping through the rain I did eventually reach Cape Wrath!)

Then, a few years ago, I was back. It was a heatwave and I'd foolishly chosen to drag the bike across from the Gairloch Road. Not on the path, mind you. I'd taken a 'short cut' and was greatly regretting it. In the middle of a tortuous maze of bog, moraine and loch, sun beating down, shoulders aching under a heavy pack, midges and flies nibbling, I could only resolve NOT to come that way again.

But I got there, eventually. The door was ajar, the porch well stocked with bogwood. Sun shone on the loch and peaks, a cuckoo called from distant trees. One or two people were staying and there were a few tents down towards the loch shore. I'd a few miles still to go but was very tempted to stop. Shenavall was as ever.

Wild flowers

It's been one of the best early Summers for wild flower displays. We are fortunate in Caithness in having a lot of land which isn't intensively farmed so that many wet and uncultivated places remain – let us preserve them!

In May, there were great purple areas of the normally sparsely growing lousewort on the hill. In early June the displays of cowslip at Strathy were phenomenal, with a range of other spring flowers that would make the gardener despair. Indeed I sometimes wonder whether all the effort spent in floral gardening might be better spent in encouraging our own native wild species.

Cycling, on a quiet road, is an excellent way of appreciating the roadside displays. A field of yellow buttercup mixed with the pink of ragged robin. A great patch of yellow flag. A ditch filled with tiny blue forgetmenot. A grass verge studded with early-purple and heath orchids.

A game I sometimes play is to spot as many different flowers as possible on the ride home from work. Flower spotting from a bike at 20 MPH can be difficult, there's no way I can identify different kinds of buttercup or speedwell. Still, on a good day at this time of year, taking the 20-mile route via Broubster, I might reach a total of 70 or so (a good botanist would double that figure). That way you soon learn where all the different varieties grow, and can watch them coming into flower day by day.

First, I make sure to admire the displays of thrift and lady's fingers before leaving site as there won't be any more on the way home (sometimes I think the Dounreay site should be made an SSSI – there is even Scottish Primrose growing just outside the fence). Also, remember to look out for a few good clumps of comfrey just before the Achreamie turn, the only place I'll see it. Immediately I'm off the main road, the flowers come thick and fast – buttercup, clover, daisy but also tormentil, orchids, cow-parsely, meadowsweet. There are the field weeds of blue and yellow vetch, there are the yellow flowers and silvery leaves of silverweed,

trying to creep across the road. There is sorrel and hawkbit, the odd dandelion, and the yellow vetch-like birds-foot trefoil.

By the wood, the first cross-leaved heath and bell-heather are out; later in the year you may see the occasional solitary white flower of Grass of Parnassus, one of our most beautiful. White bedstraw grows thickly on the banks, the pink ragged robin is scattered in the wetter places. A few large yellow flowers of greater celandine are still out in the ditches, though mostly over now; here too are the large white ox-eye daisies, which I always think of as railway weeds.

I hurtle down the hill and onto the Broubster road. Watch out carefully here, in the wetter acid bogs near the road grow flowers that won't be seen later such as red-rattle, marsh cinquefoil, the little violet-like flowers of the insectivorous butterwort, the lousewort. Gorse is out but nearly over, banks of the sweet-scented meadow-sweet are just opening. Even thistles can give a fine display when massed-there's a good patch of them – and look, a magnificent display of yellow-flag, as good as any garden plant, as I approach the bridge over the Forss.

The river's only a trickle after a long dry spell – look, there may be some yellow balsam – but nothing to match the superb displays by the burn on the Dounreay site. There's also a good display at Bridge of Westfield. Are the yellow spikes of bog ashphodel out yet? Yes, there's one, early. Nowhere else but in Caithness have I known this flower grow in thickets, an amazing sight. The air is strongly scented by the bog myrtle but this plant has no flowers visible from a bike.

The nodding heads of water avens are easily missed; there are a couple of good patches, one near Brawlbin and another by the Halkirk-Calder road. Also keep eyes peeled for some small pink willow-herb flowers, near Brawlbin. Are those little blue things speedwell or forgetmenot? I need a good headwind to slow me up so that I can see! Can I count that yellow turnip flower as wild and is the patch of blue cranesbill a garden escape? Was that a small white stitchwort in the grass?

The odd wild dog-rose makes a showing and on, past Halkirk, the massed white elder-flower is just coming out while the last of the similar-looking rowan is fading. Field weeds take over again, lots of vetch, with red dead-nettles, woundwort and field pansy showing in a week or two's time.

Where else can you have such a journey home from work? Yet there's less than there was. In Southern England they are now frantically trying to conserve what's left. Here some verges are still sprayed unnecessarily leaving a half-dead brown mess, or are far too enthusiastically cut. A few places have some SSSI protection but much is totally at the mercy of a farmer who decides to do a bit of drainage; one day's work with a JCB and another fine habitat is gone for good. Rubbish is dumped, I recently recovered several containers full of used sump oil which were floating in a pond. Everywhere in the south they are now recreating 'wild' habitats; here we are still destroying them. Conservation begins at home!

One of our great assets in Caithness is the unspoilt countryside that has mostly never been intensively farmed. Let's look after it.

Munros the hard way

Fast roads and reliable cars have superficially tamed much formerly remote Highland country. Mountains which were inaccessible, poorly mapped and only well known to long-exiled locals are now the destination of the day tripper who can't understand or pronounce the Gaelic names and doesn't realise that the empty glens were once full of people.

To drive to the foot of a peak you've never seen before, to climb it in a few hours and then drive back to the town or city is a poor way to treat a proud mountain. Here for thousands of years people lived, worked and died, herded cattle to the shieling lands, fought invaders and neighbouring clans, sheltered fugitives. The mountain was always there, a part of life. Now the main road carries coach parties past at 60MPH, people peer dopily out at another bit of Scotland, 'Munro-baggers' nip up and down to add another scalp.

The best way to approach a peak is from a hill camp, far from the roads, or else by bike. You need time to get the feel of the country from which the mountains rise, time to appreciate the gradual change of landscape as you approach.

Shortly after six in the morning I was pedalling westwards along the back road from Beauly to Cannich at the start of what was to be a 15-hour day. The narrow road is a cyclist's classic, with cars deterred by many blind bends and a faster alternative route on the other side of the river. Through the cool early morning I glided, in and out of birch and alder woods above the green river flats of Strath Glass, the air scented with bog-myrtle and pine. A buzzard mewed overhead, a roe-deer leaped across the road yards in front of me, with a clatter of frantic hooves on the tarmac.

After a very brief stretch of main road I was back in the narrow lanes, through green fields to Tomich then on up the valley westwards onto forestry roads. For miles the road climbed gently, passing near Plodda Falls – a stream, diverted in Victorian times over a 100-foot cliff. Planted forest gradually gave way to natural

pine and birch, the river became smaller and fast-running. I passed the isolated farm of Cougie (offering one of the remotest B&B's) then on for another mile till the track degenerated into a path. Nine-thirty, and the start of the proper mountains.

My destination was the Ceannacroc hills, three Munros rising to 3600 feet and usually climbed from a car parked on the busy Glenshiel road. My approach was longer, but more natural. A delightful path wended on west above Glen Affric; below could be seen the infamous Highland Cross 'Yellow Brick Road' along which I'd sweated just three weeks before. It is always nice to return to appreciate the Affric scenery at a more leisurely pace! The feeling was now of entering really remote country, as the path turned up an empty glen and came to an end near a peaty loch.

These aren't difficult hills, mostly grassy with some easily-avoided steep crags. The weather however began closing in on gaining height; there was drizzle on the first peak, cloud and rain on the second. I was glad of spare clothes and cagoule, having been too hot in shorts and T-shirt on the bike! By compass I found the correct ridge and emerged into sun again on the final plateau.

I lingered over the views of clearing hills, down to Glen Shiel, across to the Knoydart and Great Glen peaks, back the way I'd come to Glen Affric. A rough descent of the west ridge then brought me down to Coire Dho, hot in the late afternoon sun. I'd met nobody.

A recent article I'd read described how 'Munro-baggers', bound for these hills in droves, had churned the Coire Dho path into a quagmire. Where were all the hordes? There had been a little path, about a foot wide, over the tops but scarcely a blazed highway. The Coire Dho path certainly was in a mess – but not one boot-print. A nearby herd of cows, wandering freely in the Summer pastures, was to blame. This is typical of much of the hype written about pressure on the hills caused by walkers and munro-baggers and mountain bikers. I suspect most correspondents wander no further from their cars than the bar of a local hotel and listen to tall tales from the locals.

The real pressures and threats come from large scale commercial exploitation, ski developments, peat extraction, forestry, wind-farms, super-quarries. Local opinion is manipulated to permit destruction of large areas for the sake of a very few will-o-the-wisp jobs. There is room, and plenty of it, for all the small number of hillgoers braving Scotland's weather and insects!

There were still six miles to go back to the bike. A good stalkers' path led me eastwards, climbing high over the moors in the early evening sun, the corries and crags of the peaks I'd crossed in mist and rain now sunlit. The wind had dropped and the midges were waiting at the bike, so it didn't take long to set off again.

To get in a car and drive off after a day in the hills is always a painfully abrupt return to the many cares of modern life. Far better a long bike ride, through evening sun and scents, shafts of sunlight through the trees on dancing insects, the hills slowly sinking behind, a journey through the Highlands at a more natural pace. Those peaks could have been rushed in five hours from a car. Instead they formed but a small part of the day, a long slow summer day, a rare day indeed.

Fly attack

Insect life has to be a prime consideration in any outdoor activity in the Highlands during July and August. I doubt that anywhere in the world can present a more hostile environment, in that respect, than the native woodland of some northern glen such as Strathfarrar, on a still, muggy day.

A short walk through the heather leaves the legs crawling with ticks. The air is black with buzzing, sweat-sucking flies, two or three clegs are constantly diving in to attack. Stop, and the midges gather in clouds, while mosquitoes silently land and do their damage unfelt. Wasps and ants also demand attention. It's the sweat-sucking flies that are worst of all though, even though they don't bite,

Seen from the holiday cottage near Kiltarlity, the 2900-foot peak of Bha'ach Ard formed a high horizon to the north. By means of a five-mile walk from Struy, at the foot of Strathfarrar, it would be just possible to climb it after tea. So one fine evening I set off in the car, bike on the roof, and drove the ten miles to Struy. The bike would take me a further two miles past the locked gate at the foot of the glen to Culligran, allowing me to take the shortest route to the peak on foot.

Farmers were out haymaking and the hills glowed in the late, warm, sunshine. It seemed a shame not to be cycling further than Culligran on such a lovely evening. Here I set off on foot, wearing tracksuit leggings as protection from the ticks, with a hat to keep the flies off…

My plan was to walk up, fairly briskly, and jog down in the dusk. The flies had other ideas. No sooner had I started pushing through the heather and birch scrub then a great buzzing cloud gathered. I speeded up, sweated more, and more came. No midges, no clegs, a glorious Summer evening and flies by the hundred. I had seen worse though, and sweated on. Soon I'd get above them, I thought.

Above the birches the flies were just as bad. If I slowed up they gathered even more, crawling all over me. A short sprint would temporarily leave them behind,

before they gathered anew. Like a whip they drove me on, as hard as I could go, jogging up where it wasn't too steep, pouring with sweat.

The evening sun cast long shadows in the valleys stretching east to the pale blue Beauly Firth. The higher hills rose sharp into the warm, clear air. All around looked serene and beautiful – and I was sweating up steep heathery slopes surrounded by a huge black cloud of determined flies.

Waving my hat diminished the numbers briefly as each swipe collected some 20 or 30 inside – but there were always more. It was on the last grass before the summit that the numbers started falling off and only at the very top was there enough breeze to keep them all away. What a relief! The climb had taken nearly an hour less than planned.

A mile-long grassy ridge leads eastwards; along this I now jogged, enjoying the views and the fly-free serene evening light while a herd of deer and calves cantered off. I don't think anything else gives you the same sense of freedom as jogging along a high mountain ridge late on a summer evening.

After a last lingering look at the view I slid down a small remaining patch of July snow and commenced the run back. It was now 9.30PM, the sun had left the lower slopes and the flies had vanished, just like that. The four miles down were heavenly compared to the climb up, in spite of much rough and wet going, and the cool late evening gloaming gave a pleasant cycle back to the car.

The next day was hotter and we decided to outsmart the insects by cheating. We drove through the heat to Aviemore and took the chair-lift up to 3700 feet on Cairngorm. As a purist I deplore (of course) the mess made of these hills in the name of skiing. But how nice, after the previous evening's struggle, to drive to 2000 feet and then be lifted effortlessly up into the relatively cool air of the plateau.

Floating gently upwards, we looked down on three young men, heavily laden, who had for some reason chosen a route of ascent directly below the chair-lift and sweated uphill each surrounded by his own black cloud. Two had coats over their heads in a forlorn attempt to keep the insects off. I knew how they felt.

Even at the top of the chair-lift there were flies and the continual stream of people climbing the eroded path to Cairngorm summit acted as a fly escalator, delivering cloud after cloud to the summit cairn which was buzzing with them in spite of drifting mist and a breeze.

We only had to walk a few hundred yards to the north-west, however, to leave nearly all the flies and all the tourists behind. A cool breeze blew pleasantly, yet down in the glens it would be baking. We sauntered across the bare plateau to find a spectacular view down to Loch Avon, then wandered back round the side of Cairngorm, passing, to the youngster's delight, a small snowfield. We saw Alpine flowers and a baby mountain hare and almost NO flies (or people) till nearly back at the chair-lift.

Leave the Highland Summer insects out of your plans at your peril!

Ben Armine and Kinbrace

Ben Armine is one of the remotest peaks in Scotland. Unless you have permission and a Land-Rover, the round walk to the southern-most peak of Creag Mhor involves a walk of at least 25 miles.

A much better route than a long tramp down the Loch Choire or Ben Armine Lodge track is to traverse the heart of the Sutherland flow country, crossing the remote valley of the River Skinsdale. So at 7.15 one early July morning I left the train at Kildonan, bound for a walk of over 30 miles. My aim was to cross Creag Mhor, possibly then carrying on to Lairg to pick up the late train north. This would mean walking nearly 40 miles and time would be very short; more likely was a return to Kinbrace which would allow me an extra hour.

The day was ideal for walking, cool and clear but cloud keeping the sun off and a breeze to keep the midges down. A track, following the pylons, led me over a low col to Craggie, a typical deserted and ruinous croft, with an empty and little-used lodge nearby. Every step westward now took me into remoter and remoter country.

The track soon came to an end and the next 30 miles were almost entirely pathless. Up grassy slopes to the low moorland hill of Cnoc Tuarie then into typical rough flow-country terrain of tussock, bog and dubh-loch which was to dominate much of the walk. I'm well used to the open spaces of Caithness but the spaciousness of this country is even more impressive. Miles and miles of empty, rolling moor, no fences, paths, masts, a real tundra landscape. Ben Armine looked a long, long way off.

Below the top of the northern peak there could be seen a small patch of snow; a very unusual feature so late in the year and visible from Caithness until mid-July. I'd hoped to visit it, but even the 13 hours between trains didn't give enough time.

On, westward, for mile after mile I tramped over the bogs of this vast rolling landscape. At last came the green valley of the Skinsdale, and the prominent ruined croft of Cnocan. Gable ends, nettles and a broken cast iron leg of a 'Singer' sewing machine. This must have been one of the remotest crofts in the Highlands but then the nearest neighbour would have been only about three miles away, by the Black Water, with Rowena Farre's croft (of 'Seal Morning' fame) a couple of miles further on.

There was still a long way to go. Passing the old peat banks (at least the croft had fuel on its doorstep) and a lochan with wailing diver, I trudged on towards Creag Mhor. It took another hour to reach the shores of grey Gorm Loch Mhor, below steep broken slopes. An eagle soared along the hillside, disappearing out of sight to the north. Setting my face to the hill, steep ground unfamiliar after the long moorland walk, I sweated upwards, emerging onto the mossy plateau and the cairn some six hours after leaving Kildonan. Alas, not enough time to carry on to Lairg, but time to savour the view across a real 'Last Great Wilderness' before starting the long trek back to Kinbrace.

It was after hours of bog and moorland walking that, with some relief, I reached the end of a good track at Altanduin, on Michael Wigan's Borrobol estate. Yet another sadly deserted farm, a collection of buildings in various states of decay and disuse, now easily accessible by landrover and quad with no need for people to live there. It was nice though to see a bit of conservation fencing, with a few patches of old natural woodland protected from the deer and now regenerating thickly.

The wind was dying and the midges rising as I tramped on eastward along a good track, enjoying the luxury of being able to look around without watching my feet all the time. Evening light coming on, another two hours to my train at Kinbrace. I turned off the track, crossed the hill and river, and climbed up past a very fine ruined broch to a moorland top overlooking the river Helmsdale. This whole area is littered with prehistoric cairns and settlements; only in the last couple of hundred years has it gone to grass and deer and sheep.

The Helmsdale River was low, and easy to ford; a walk along its grassy banks soon brought me into Kinbrace, with half an hour to spare.

Kinbrace is the smallest of villages, and has a certain frontier atmosphere about it. The first thing I noticed at the approach to the village was a small corrugated iron hut, with a notice attached. This turned out to be the local Kirk, with the Helmsdale minister visiting monthly to take the service. The theme for the year, proudly announced, was – 'Back to Basics'. Just a hundred yards on was a garage, with possibly the oldest petrol pumps in the north. Some of the cars parked nearby had been there a while; one had grass growing out from the radiator grill.

It was a fine Summer Saturday evening. Everything was quiet, nobody was about. I walked onto the platform to check the train time – due in 25 minutes – and into the shelter for a sandwich away from the midges. Here, lay a roll of newspapers, bound in string, indeed all the Kinbrace Saturday papers, in a wrapper addressed to the wee shoppy across from the station, presumably to be collected by their readers on Sunday or Monday morning. The selection ranged from the Morning Star to Lloyd's List and the Financial Times. A cosmopolitan place, Kinbrace. I was very tempted to take one out, HALF do the crossword and put it back but decided I'd better not.

I pottered up through the village to the main Helmsdale road; it only took five minutes. Here was a neat cottage with immaculate potatoes and brassicas growing in the garden. The name on the gate? 'Dunstalkin'. Just opposite was a real crofters' house, complete as usual with a couple of rusting old cars. An unusual method of disposal had however been adopted; they were being buried. Turf almost covered both of them, just a few gaps remained.

A place with character, Kinbrace. Barely 12 eagle miles from Ben Armine, 12 train hours from London. The sort of place where I wouldn't mind living myself!

Wet day on Foinaven

You can't win 'em all. What, after all, can you expect on a walk through the wettest area in the North during an unsettled spell of weather? I planned a long day, traversing the whole Foinaven ridge and possibly taking in Arkle. So I was driving west from Thurso before six in the morning, not too worried by the rain which had been falling for some hours and so should soon clear.

In August the north coast road is best taken early, before the tourists have woken up. It was empty, and as the rain-soaked moors and lochans passed I listened to at least three weather forecasts. A low was crossing Northern Scotland, which sounded bad, however all were in agreement that the rain would soon give way to brighter skies with showers.

A deluge in StrathNaver did not herald an improvement, nor did steady rain over the Moin and low cloud around Eribol. It was not yet eight when I set off on foot from the southern end of the loch up the grey wet slopes of Cranstackie. There were 14 hours of daylight; plenty of time for the weather to improve.

To climb Foinaven from this, the most interesting side, requires an initial crossing of the south ridge of Cranstackie. The slopes here rise at a gentle angle from the sea-loch, a bare landscape of rock-slab, boulder and short heather. Ominously, the rivers were already high, tumbling white out of the low cloud.

With careful route-finding it was an easy walk up to the ridge crest at about 1400 feet. Here, the spectacular corries of Foinaven open up across the deep gulf of Strath Dionard, unless hidden by cloud and rain, as they were now. No indication of a clearance, indeed a near gale, funnelling up the strath, was driving cold rain into my face.

I scrambled down the steep slopes to the river Dionard, a thousand feet below. It had that 'rising fast' look to it, grasses submerged but not flattened, an oily smooth surface, uninviting to cross. A salmon leaped with a splash, further downstream some fishermen were already out. I dithered up and down the banks

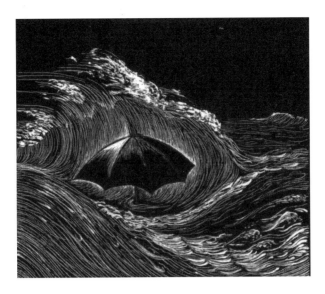

for a few minutes before finally plunging in; it was in fact only about two feet deep though fast flowing and I made it across without a salmon leaping into my arms.

Water was pouring out of the Foinaven corries. I followed one white river up to a wild lochan, then on up to a landscape of boulder and rock slab, swept by the rain below quartzite crags. In the shelter of a huge boulder I ate an early lunch, before pushing on to where the final steep slopes rose into the cloud. The wind had risen and the rain was heavier than ever, my lightweight waterproofs were letting in water and I was wearing all my clothes. I'd have brought better equipment if such weather had been anticipated. A traverse of the ridge was not going to be possible, also the River Dionard might need a big detour on the way back. It was time to retreat.

An interesting walk was still possible. Skirting the end of the quartzite ridge I came down where a river, pouring out of the next corry to the north, roared down a 50-foot waterfall. Crossing with some difficulty below, I made my way down to the shores of Loch Dionard, under the spectacular 1000-foot crags of Creag Urbhard. This is one of the finest spots in the North, particularly on a wild day when waterfalls seam the crags. Some almost evaporate into mist, like miniature Angel Falls, while one large torrent roars down a number of high steps and gorges. I'd love to see it when everything is in real spate – the difficulty would be in getting there!

On the loch was a boat. Fishing that loch in such a setting must be superb on a nice day, but to sit on a loch, soaked and frozen, lashed by driving rain… no doubt the fishermen thought the lone walker equally stupid. At least I wasn't having to pay for my 'pleasure'.

After picking my way along the shore and crossing the side rivers there was still the obstacle of the main river, even if a few miles nearer its source. Finding a spot where it was split by an island I waded in; the current nearly swept me away but it was possible – just. Another hour and I'd have had to detour miles around its headwaters.

There were still many wet miles to go back to the car, first over a low bealach above Loch Dionard then down a little path to Strath Beag followed by a long trudge out. The River Beag was overflowing its banks necessitating several detours, I waded waist deep through sluggish side rivers. Once wet you don't get any wetter! At last the car, at 5.30 PM, a change into dry clothes, a flask of hot tea – great!

I listened with interest to the weather forecast as I drove homewards through the rain. No apologies. 'The heavy rain in the Far North will continue for a few hours before clearing slowly.' You can't win 'em all.

An August day in the Far North

An August day in the Far North. The sun rises at 5.30 over the edge of the moor, throwing a shadow from the croft-house a quarter of a mile down the fields. Dew glistens, anyone abroad this early sees a white halo refracted around the shadow of their head. Early sun gleams on distant hill and mountain slopes, Knockfin, Armine, Klibreck, briefly Summer-green and sharp in the clear air.

Midges gather round the moorland sheep, they toss their heads and flick their ears, eating hurriedly and moving on to the next, greener, tuft. There is yet little wind. The low sun shines over great drifts of heavily scented meadow-sweet by the roadsides, here and there mixed with the red of willow-herb or ragged robin. Miles of quiet verges have been lined with white for weeks, first cow-parsley, then hogweed, now ground-elder and meadowsweet.

The creel-boat is setting out from the harbour, wind is forecast for later. Little waves lap the white shell-sand beach, across the bay are the red cliffs of Dunnet Head, beyond are the rounded hills of Hoy. Terns fuss, piping oyster-catchers fly low. Along the low clifftops the odd late flower of pink thrift is still in bloom, with patches of wild thyme, while the oyster plant with its fleshy leaves and bright blue flowers sprawls over slabby rocks near the sea. A few yards inland, dense thickets of hogweed and nettle give way suddenly to the short grass of cultivation where hay has been cut and baled.

The creel boatman hauls in the night's catch, Lobsters and crabs are now scarce as a result of over-fishing by large operators. But it's a way of life. Half a mile away a tractor sweeps up swathes of cut grass to deposit round bales every 50 yards, making silage while the sun shines.

It's not yet eight. From the 'Hoy View Lounge', the lorry-driver crossing to Orkney on the 'St Ola' sees the 1200-foot cliffs of Hoy slipping past the window, he smokes a last cigarette over coffee before getting ready to disembark at Stromness. It's been a good smooth voyage. Meanwhile, 60 miles further south, the refreshments trolley makes its third trip along the early-morning train as it rattles down the raised beaches to Brora. Seals and cormorants bask on the rocks and an early golfer tees off on the links.

Curtains in the house are tightly drawn against the bright sun, for some it is still night. Baby rabbits nibble on the roadside by fields of ripening barley. The oats look, as ever, as if they'll not quite make it. Bumble-bees fly to and fro in the garden, potatoes are growing, gooseberries and currants are ripening, carrots are ready for eating, soon too the peas and broccoli.

From the bakery a smell of chocolate-cake drifts out across the town, from the B&B the smell of frying bacon. On the crowded campsite the first camping gas stoves and Primus stoves are hissing, sleepy caravanners goggle at the view across the blue sea to the sharp, sunlit hills of Hoy.

Six buses in a row, several hundred cars one, two, three, overtaking, 60–70MPH, nine miles in ten minutes. The Dounreay rush is on, from bed to plant or office in 25 minutes, pop music or news of the latest war on car radio. A young herring-gull lies dead in the road, each car in turn veers to miss it. Down, over the bridge, round. Under the bridge the river flows quietly, the waterfall little more than a trickle. Salmon jump in the bay, awaiting the rains.

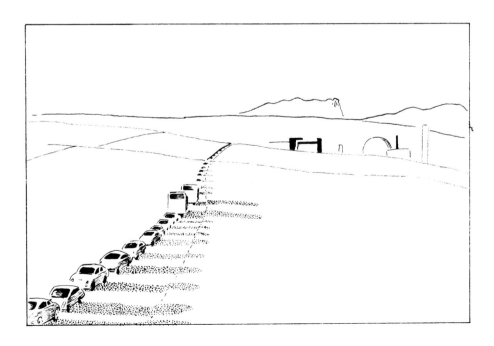

The morning draws on. Bumble-bees fly to and fro in the garden. There's a light breeze from the south-east and a bit more haze, now its getting really warm. Shops are busy, the Co-op car-park is full, the trolley queues are lengthening. The tourist caravans and caravettes are on their way, to stop and start and pull in and out of passing places all the way to Tongue and Durness. A piper plays to the crowds at John O' Groats.

Blue and brown butterflies flutter over the flowery east coast slopes – harebell, Grass of Parnassus, bedstraw , yellow rattle. Honey-suckle clings to the cliff-top. A family of eider ducks, the young now well grown, waddle into the sea from the empty, stony beach. Anemones wave pink fronds in rock pools. Puffins fly to and from their burrows on the stack. The last of the young kittiwakes, black and white, take to the air from the ledges.

The moorland deer are restless, pursued by clegs and clouds of flies. A rare family of grouse feeds in the heather. The keeper, hopeful for the twelfth, is out counting the meagre numbers, buzzing up the shallow grassy strath in his all-terrain quad. The peat is already stacked. Dragonflies dart over dubh-lochs. Diver-chicks are now hatched, but one of the pair succumbed to the arctic skuas which nested nearby, the remaining chick swims close to its parents. Suddenly the peace is smashed by the screech and roar of a pair of low-flying jets, just ten minutes out of Lossiemouth. Nothing takes the slightest bit of notice. The quiet descends again.

Bell-heather and cross-leaved heath are in full bloom with early ling on sunny banks. Soon the road from Loch More to Dalnawhillan and Glutt Lodge will be lined with purple and scented with honey for all its 12 miles.

Now the south-east wind is strengthening, cold mist drifts in and out of Wick. Further west the wind, blowing over miles of sun-baked moor is hot. The afternoon sun, beating on flat office roofs at Dounreay raises indoor temperatures to the mid-eighties. With blinds drawn against the sun and doors propped open, desk workers sweat at computer screens. On the foreshore, great banks of yellow balsam soak up the afternoon sun. Between John O'Groats and Burwick the wind is a good force seven, against the tide, the sea is turning wild and chaotic. Day-trip tourists to Orkney on the 'Pentland Venture' will have an interesting return crossing.

Evening draws on. Westward the sun lowers through the haze of smoke carried from cities hundreds of miles to the south, before disappearing behind thick high cloud. Over much of Caithness the air is now fresh and cool, with haar still lingering on the east coast. Hooked cirrus clouds are moving in overhead. At Armadale and Bettyhill the wind has dropped, the air is warm, humid and sticky. Midges swarm, tourists seal themselves inside tent or caravan. The rain is spotting in Tongue, there's cloud on Ben Loyal. Ten miles west and Foinaven is lashed by wind and driving rain, the Dionard is high, the salmon are jumping. In Strath Hope the campers cower out of the wind and rain. Thick fog and drizzle shroud Cape Wrath.

Nights are starting to draw in, by 10PM dusk settles over Caithness. The tractor is still out on the hill, headlights blazing, the farmer will be baling till midnight. It's still dry in the east, but rain is forecast. A neighbour is flattening silage in the clamp, driving the tractor up and down and up and down, making the day as long as is has to be. Old cars and taxis throng the streets of the town, youngsters gather, catcalls come and go. The 'Ola' slips into Scrabster harbour after its sixth crossing of the Pentland Firth, a little late with the strong winds. Two trawlers are setting out. Peat reek drifts from the croft chimney. Curtains are drawn, lights are out – already night for some. An August day in the Far North.

Remotest north-west

The far north-west of Sutherland holds some of the most rugged and remote country in the British Isles. Perhaps the least known area is the range of high hills west of Gobernuisgeach Lodge, near the Hope Lodge-Altnaharra road, itself one of the remotest strips of tarmac on the mainland. The highest peak, over 2600 feet, has one of the longest names – Meallan Liath Coire Mhic Dhughaill – and rises above an austere corrie loch defended on all sides by a tangle of rocky hills and bouldery peaty pathless glens. Rugged, rough country, the Highlands at their best, and within day return distance of Caithness – just.

I set off at 6.30 on the Scottish Bank Holiday Monday and drove the empty roads for two hours to a spot about half-way between Hope Lodge and Altnaharra. It was grey and a bit showery but not looking bad at all for one of our wettest Augusts; there was even the possibility that the sun might make a showing.

By the time I'd splashed two miles across soggy moor, waded a couple of full rivers and wended my way up between the grey rock slabs to the ridge of Beinn Direach, the rain was lashing down. The ridges, once you've gained them, give the best walking, often gentle with grass, moss and patches of bare stones, while the glens are a tangled morass of peat hags, interspersed with moraines and broken rock.

As I neared the summit of Direach the rain eased off and the view opened up again to the north, down Strath Hope to Loch Eribol, but with cloud still sullenly over Ben Hope.

The next peak, Carn an Tionail was temporarily clear ahead of an approaching shower and I hurried down bouldery slopes and up steep grass between slabs to the top for a brief view of my planned destination, still three arduous miles away.

The hills here cradle some superb lochans in rocky basins. Unvisited and peaceful, they reflect the blue of heaven on a fine day and embody the essence of the remotest Scottish Highlands in the grey and wet. I ate my sandwiches by a rocky shore, mist and sheeting rain came and went with even, as I set off again, a glimpse of blue sky.

The circuit of the high ridges around Coire Loch is one of the great walks of the Far North and it was a pity that there was little to see. The rain came down, harder and heavier, the wind blew and the cloud only lifted enough for the odd brief glimpse of the grey loch below. It wasn't even worth detouring to the highest point and instead I took a short cut down steep slopes to the more sheltered corry.

The rain had set in for the rest of the afternoon. I picked my way down the slippery slopes below the loch outlet to the wilderness of peat and moraine at the head of the glen where three waterfalls tumbling white down rocky slides meet. It was four miles of rough and slow going down the glen in the beating rain and another three on paths and tracks back to the car – a long day, but an experience of remote north-west Sutherland to savour.

Walks in Caithness

'Can you suggest where we might go for a walk in Caithness?' It's a question I'm asked from time to time and a difficult one to answer, there being so many possibilities! Let me here suggest a few ideas.

All the Caithness coast is worth walking, a few of the best stretches come immediately to mind: Follow the shore from Dunbeath to the castle. Walk south from the Old Man of Wick, along the clifftops to Sarclet. Walk the length of Sinclairs Bay (paddling through the river Wester, halfway along) and return along the links. The clifftops at Duncansby are fenced and a good place to go with small children to see the cliff nesting birds, the clifftop flowers, the stacks and geos. Circuit the whole of Dunnet Head along the clifftops; start at Dunnet and finish by walking back along the road from Brough. Walk west from Reay, round Sandside Head, to the Sutherland border (and on to the Halladale). All the dozens of little bays and geos down the east coast are worth visiting in their own right.

There are many good river walks. The Thurso can be followed, on either bank, most of the way from source to sea. Perhaps the best stretches are at Dirlot, and between Westerdale and Halkirk. The Forss is good, particularly north from Loch Shurrery, between Forss and Crosskirk, and south-west from Bridge of Westfield. It's a nice walk up the River Wick from the sea to Loch Watten, a walk that is much more interesting than you'd expect from the roads and gives you a completely new impression of the country. The Dunbeath Water gives one of the best and most famous walks, from Dunbeath just keep going along the north bank as far as you feel like (and come back over Morven if you wish!). The Langwell and Berriedale Waters, both real mountain rivers, give grand walks along most of their lengths.

Most Caithness hills make up in interest for what they lack in altitude. Dorrery Hill from the lodge, or much better from the old Brawlbin school, is well worth doing, as in Beinn Ratha from Reay. Surprisingly few people know of the beech

woods and lanes of Olrig, above Castletown; walk to the top of Olrig Hill from here, or from Hilliclay, for a view over the whole county. Spittal Hill gives an even better panorama, there is a good path from Dunn to Banniskirk and you can reach the top from here or, more easily, from the main road. Ben Alisky is a little-known moorland hill – a day's walk for the more experienced from Loch More. Morven and Scaraben deserve respect as real mountains but either is within reach of any healthy person on a fine day, the easiest approach is from Braemore. A walk over both with all the intervening tops makes an excellent hill day for the fitter walker.

The 'flow country' has always been around but only recently have ordinary people begun to appreciate its real value. To get a flavour of it, walk up onto Blar Nam Faoileag from Dirlot (don't forget your map and compass). The Knockfin Heights on the Sutherland border are unique; an incredible maze of dubh loch and bog, but not for the novice. The long estate track leading west from Loch Shurrery is one of the best places from which to see and appreciate the flow country without actually having to leave the track. Detour to the top of either of the Beinn Nam Bads for a magnificent panorama of wildest Caithness. The more experienced can make a longer round walk by cutting across the moors to Loch

Caluim, walking back east along the track to Dorrery and returning to the starting point by following the eastern shore of Loch Shurrery or crossing Dorrery Hill.

Sea, river, mountain and moor – and then the other feature where Caithness excels – loch. You may never climb all the Munros but how about visiting all the Caithness lochs? (or better still swimming in or fishing all of them!) A walk along the shore of Loch Calder or Loch Watten is always worthwhile. But my favourites are the remote moorland lochs with sandy beaches; I'm not naming them here – go and find them! Loch More is however almost as good. You can drive to it and then wander along its sandy shores for a mile or two; it's particularly recommended on a frosty Winter day. Loch Stemster, by the Lybster road should be walked right round with a visit to the nearby stone circle and also to the ruined village of Badryrie with its secret room where home-made whisky was produced. Then there is Loch of Yarrows where the ground is littered with standing and fallen stones, cairns and brochs and you could spend days exploring. Some of the smallest lochs are some of the best – Loch of Warehouse, Loch a Mhuillinn, the Reay Binocular Lochs for example.

Whenever I look at the map fresh ideas come to mind. I'm always finding somewhere new to walk, something I didn't know was there. The other day there were a couple of hundred square yards of grass covered in what looked like daisies. But the flowers were Grass of Parnassus. Such discoveries are commonplace in Caithness. The difficulty with planning a walk is in having too much choice!

Morven by bike

Robert Dick walked from Thurso to the summit of Morven and back within 24 hours; a walk which others have managed in more recent times. It's a nice idea to climb the highest Caithness peak without annihilating the distance in a car, but a 60-mile walk is a bit much for me. Instead I took the easier option of cycling it.

Midges, clegs and clammy weather mean that, in late August, the hills are really best left to the grouse-shooters and deer-stalkers who pay for the privilege of being eaten alive in the sweaty heat. A fine day with light winds was forecast however, it sounded ideal for cycling.

It was bright and calm but too cold for shorts as I pedalled off towards Spittal. The sun was hidden by a band of cloud to the south which gradually moved in to give one of those humid, rather cloudy days which midges love. On a bike you keep sweeping them up on arms and legs and even as the day warmed up, shorts and a T-shirt just could not be worn.

The Causewaymire is a road that's great to cycle in the calm or a following wind but purgatory in a strong headwind. It was an enjoyable, fast ride. Loch Rangag looked idyllic, mirror-calm, a few ripple-rings from rising fish – looks can be deceptive! Farmers were out early, gathering sheep for a sale at Dunbeath – you could see from the characteristic way they kept walking about and wiping their faces that it wasn't a morning for hanging around.

On the Braemore road out of Dunbeath two men were working fast and jerkily, loading peat into a trailer, again pausing ever so often to wipe their faces and heads... Somebody had pitched a tent right by the river at Braemore in a picture-book spot. But to choose such a site in late August they couldn't be Scots. Sure enough, two campers were sitting in an English registration car eating breakfast with the windows tightly closed, no doubt wondering how they were going to get their tent packed up. I lifted the bike over the gate and pedalled off quickly before the biters had time to gather.

From Braemore you can cycle, on right-of-way tracks, right through to Glutt Lodge and out to Loch More and Westerdale, a highly recommended route. The mountains were ahead, enticingly clear under a bright, dappled sky.

After a couple of miles the track forks, the right-hand branch heading for Glutt. I detoured left and bumped along for another couple of miles until opposite Morven. All was still and calm, nobody was out after either grouse or deer. So I left the bike and splashed down through the bogs and across the river. An hour later and I was on the summit of Morven. The view on a clear day never fails to impress, with the whole of Caithness visible as on a map, also much of Sutherland and some of Orkney. Distant peaks stretched to south of Ullapool; on the clearest days you can see the Cairngorms and possibly even Ben Nevis down the Great Glen.

Unfortunately there was only the odd puff of wind to dispel the midges which had been carried up on the warm updrafts, it's a bit much when they spoil a well-earned contemplative rest on a mountain summit! I ate lunch back at the bike where the combination of a light breeze and lots of insect repellent made things bearable.

The track across to Glutt has one of the smoothest surfaces of moorland roads and views are not obscured by great mounds of dug-out peat as in the new forests . It provides one of the best of moorland bike rides. The midges were keeping everyone indoors at Glutt Lodge, the remotest dwelling in the county, with not even a dog barking as I passed. For the next nine miles I bumped over stones and potholes, getting increasingly sore. At one point I didn't see a coiled adder beside the track till I'd nearly ridden over its tail – and didn't stop to investigate further!

We cyclists are soft these days, used to smooth tarmac, and it was with considerable relief that I reached the public road near Loch More. Back home, Morven looked as far away as ever. It made a good day out by bike, but I wouldn't care to emulate Robert Dick.

Three houses

Time hangs lightly, here. A newspaper dated 1977 lies folded on the table, still waiting to light the fire. Names signed in pencil on the wall in 1925 are fresher than those scrawled in ball-point pen 50 years later. It is, perhaps, two years since I was last here but immediately I'm in the door it could have been yesterday. There have been few other visitors.

The house stands little more than two miles from the end of the road. Shepherds lived here, children were born and played here, men and women died here. The house was left to moulder back into the moor, of no use to the owner in the days of Landrovers and quads.

Yet someone has been patching broken windows, sweeping up, keeping one room clean, tidy and welcoming for those who may wander this way. There is a chair, a table, a wooden bunk to sleep on. The door has a latch to keep the Winter storms from throwing it open and filling the house with snow and sheep. There's a small supply of tea and sugar, a few matches and candles.

The track, which had already been wet and overgrown with rushes vanishes totally into the bogs in places over the next mile. Even on a fine day, anyone unused to the Caithness moors could have difficulty here. Yet strings of laden ponies must have regularly come this way for, another mile further on, overlooking a large, sandy-shored trout loch, is a long, low house. The moors roll on for miles to distant mountain heights. Greylags call and fuss, a large herd of deer moves slowly off. A strange place for a house, a strange place indeed.

A conservatory-cum-porch has mostly collapsed leaving roofing irons precariously balanced over the door. There is an old china sink here; 50 years ago somebody didn't bother to do the washing up and left the dirty dishes in it. They remained there until a few years ago when the roof fell in on them...

The door is stiff, you force it open and step into a corridor running the length of the house with perhaps ten rooms opening off it. The floor sags under your tread, holes show the bare rock and peat beneath. In the first room is a bath –

and a WC! All covered in dirt, bits of plaster, pigeon droppings. The last flush was probably before the Second World War.

The next room had been a kitchen. The floor is littered with rubbish – bits of cloth, old cans, broken crockery. There is a mouldy table and a mouldering, broken chair. Cupboard doors hang open revealing rusty empty biscuit tins and tea caddies. Corroded bits of paraffin lamps litter the shelves. The stove is still there with pipes to a hot-water tank which still sits on beams near the ceiling. This place had all mod cons!

The other rooms contain an assortment of broken beds and cabinets, mouldy chairs, rusty mirrors, water-less washbasins and baths. In one cupboard is a small stack of plates, the top one thick with grime but those underneath clean enough to eat off.

One of the end rooms has, on a wall, a pencilled tally of July fishing catches, with dates, numbers and weights. The tally is dated 1903. Yet there is nothing unfriendly or sinister about the house. You could spend a comfortable night, with a sleeping bag, in one of the end rooms. Just sad – the house was built at great effort in a remote, beautiful spot – used for a time, and then abandoned. A few people and a few weekends could work wonders here; this building could be saved, a unique bothy and a haven for the few lovers of the wild and lonely places who pass this way. With the owner's permission – a job for the Mountain Bothies Association perhaps?

A few miles walk across pathless moor takes you to the third house and a good track which brings you in two miles to the road. Until recently this house was lived in, then used in the Summer and in the Autumn stalking season. There was a generator, lights, basic and comfortable furniture. As I came down from the moor I noticed that the door, which had always been locked, was open. I went in. Once again rubbish, dirt, pigeon droppings, fallen plaster everywhere. Old magazines and children's comics were scattered about. A large teddy-bear lay on the floor and a child's abacus stood by a broken window, the torn curtains flapping in the breeze.

In London, garages have sold for tens of thousands of pounds. In Caithness fine houses set in magnificent moorland scenery lie abandoned, nobody wants them, nobody cares. It's a strange world.

Views for 50 miles

Did you know that you can see the Cairngorms from the Causewaymire? Or the Cape Wrath hills from the Thurso-Dounreay Road? Probably you were more concerned about the car in front!

Distant views are, to me, fascinating. I've almost always lived in a house on a hill and start feeling claustrophic if I can't see horizons 30 or more miles away. Perhaps it's that glimpse of another, totally different, world, the childhood romance of 'over the hills and far away'. The leap of the eye to a distant mountain takes the imagination into another land.

Whenever I've lived in built-up areas I've become expert at knowing the precise spot to look out from the top deck of a bus and see, through a gap in the houses, on a rare clear day, some remote blue outline perhaps 40 or 50 miles distant. Instant escapism! Then one day I climb that distant peak on an equally clear day and see, far off, the chimneys of the city – and know I identified the right mountain.

Identification can be surprisingly difficult and direction indicators are often wrong, or omit the most interesting hill of all. You can think you know a view and then one day, in unusual light perhaps of setting or rising sun, or in snow, you realise that you can see a hill you never knew was there. Indeed, you are then probably the only person who has ever realised that you can actually see from that particular B to this particular A!

As I set out to work on the bike on a clear day, I look across the moors to the familiar outlines of Scaraben and Morven, lit perhaps by early sun. Through the gap between Morven and Carn Mor can be seen what I thought for years was Cnoc na Maoile, above the Strath of Kildonan and then discovered was actually Ben Bhealaich, above Helmsdale (see what I mean?)

Above the graceful curves of Ben Alisky and Beinn Glas-choire rises the quartzite ridge of Small Mount, with just to the left a glimpse of Creag Scalabsdale, the

third highest, and probably least visited, of Caithness mountains. Next comes the rounded hump of Cnoc an Eireannaich, one of the sources of the Kildonan gold, and then the long almost straight line of Cnoc Coire na Fearna and the Knockfin Heights. These are hills every bit as remote and mysterious as they appear!

The nearby hill of Dorrery breaks the skyline; beyond are the twin tops of the Griams and over the flowland hills of Beinn Nam Bad Mor and Beag, rises Ben Klibreck, one of the highest peaks in Sutherland, often streaked with snow. Further west, Ben Loyal thrusts its serrated ridge into the clear morning air and a few puffs of cloud drift on Ben Hope. Foinaven hides shyly behind Beinn Ratha, above Reay, but its companions, Spionnaidh and Cranstackie are clearly visible, all of 50 miles away, on the other side of Loch Eribol. The crinkly crest of Ben Hutig, above Tongue, just breaks the Shebster skyline, as does the Telecom mast above Bettyhill...

Parallax moves the skyline surprisingly fast as I pedal along the road; Scalabsdale pops fully into view and a slice of Ben Armine appears by Dorrery. Next, Foinaven slides out from behind Beinn Ratha – but now the view opens out to the north. There is Hoy, with the Old Man and, further right, Wideford Hill above Kirkwall on the Orkney Mainland.

The views are hidden on the dip into Thurso but if you take the main road west, the Sutherland skyline comes suddenly into view once you pass the top of Scrabster Brae, stunningly so if the air is clear and the hills white with snow. Now you can see more of Ben Hutig, with its high Northern cliffs dropping eight-hundred feet into the sea, and further west to the hills near Cape Wrath, 60 miles away.

There is more to see of Orkney Mainland, out to the Kitchener Memorial cliffs and, from the Achreamie Road, you can see all the way to the Brough of Birsay.

Refraction, on very clear cold mornings or evenings can cause normally hidden hills to pop into view, then is the time to see 70 miles to Ben More Assynt, Sutherland's highest, from Olrig Hill, or to glimpse Ben Hee rising just above the nearer skyline to the south of Ben Hope.

The delight of distant views is the delight of picking out the spire of St Magnus Cathedral (with binoculars) from Dunnet Head, of seeing Morven from the Cairngorms, of noticing from an office window the tiny white sliver of the very top of snow-covered Ben Hope showing above the Drumholiston hills. Ah well, you may say, on a clear day you can often see the moon! But then do you know where to look in order to see, on a clear night, the Andromeda galaxy, all of two million light years away?

The Caithness garden

I see a lot of Morven, the Griams, Ben Hope and Ben Loyal at this time of year. Not to mention Dorrery, the Knockfin Heights and Ben Klibreck. Mostly, though, without venturing more than a few yards from my front door. I live in a house on top of a hill, with a large garden.

I seem to have acquired something of a reputation for relishing the worst of weathers in the great outdoors. The truth is that, like everyone else, I'd rather be on the hills on a clear day with sun and drifting white cumulus than in a gale of driving rain. However fine weather tends to be reserved for the much more important activity of looking after the garden.

The house, when we bought it, stood in a large, unfenced patch of grass, 'garden ground' is the term. The farmer's cattle and sheep would occasionally leak out of the fields and browse around. One cow nearly calved in front of our dining room window (yes, we were having dinner at the time) pursued, with a hoof sticking out of its rear end, by the farmer.

We put up a fence, rebuilt the dry-stane dyke and hacked the tussocky grass down, over a period of weeks, with a pair of shears. We bought some gardening books and a large 'Challenge' brand notebook. Gardening at 400 feet above sea-level on the North coast of Scotland is a challenge indeed. And I'd never even grown tatties. About then, too, we discovered that you can't buy young carrot plants from the garden centre.

I started digging up the grass for flower and vegetable beds. It soon became apparent that the soil was mostly not of the best. In places the turf was straight on top of the rocky pan, and to dig to a depth of the spade took about an hour per square metre, with a ton or so of stone to remove. Mostly the soil consisted of solid clay and slugs. Another part of the garden was composed of the buried remains of fallen dry-stane dyke mixed with decades of sand washed off the road. Here too was the spot where some farmer had dumped lime, large lumps

still appearing every year. Another area had been meant for hard-standing, grassed over but desperate to dig and with loads of small stones to sieve. A pile of stones, overgrown with coltsfoot, was to form the centre of a vegetable plot. Over the years I must have barrowed in at least 50 tons of manure.

One square of grass was left wild, to remind us how things used to look. Every year it produces a fine crop of purple orchids, as well as vetch, cow parsley, the odd bluebell and a sea of waving grass. Very fashionable now!

We collected a load of little trees and planted them, in what we later found was the best soil in the garden and should really have been the vegetable patch. Carefully nurtured, those which were relatively local strains are still growing 20 years later, alder, hazel, sycamore, whitebeam, rowan, birch, holly, even beech. Slow growing perhaps, but trees can be grown even on an exposed Caithness hilltop!

Digging and manuring the soil are jobs I enjoy in the Winter. Take a gale of sleet on a Sunday afternoon, fit for nothing else but dressing up in waterproofs and barrowing manure from a heap in the field, 200 yards away. Fifteen minutes a load, dragging the laden barrow through the mud, watching the winter dusk fall – then in for a cup of tea by the fire. Digging – I'll dig in any weather, the wetter the better. The soil's so heavy that a bit of water makes little difference and it makes another good job for a wind and rain-lashed Winter afternoon.

A friend of mine once reckoned that cutting his grass was equivalent in effort to climbing a Munro. This seemed ridiculous but then it occurred to me that I could be up and down Ben Hope in much less time than it takes to cut all the grass when it is long and wet. The secret, as with any gardening, is to take things easy, to stop at the end of the row of digging or mowing, look at the view, listen to the birds, admire the flowers you've spent so much effort growing and weeding. The great thing about a garden in the country is that you can enjoy the scenery, the birdsong, the great open skies of Caithness in between planting the brocolli or thinning the carrots.

It took a few years to realise just how marginal things are here for gardening. The season is two or three weeks shorter than even in Thurso or Wick, and the exposure to wind vastly greater. Every year a few gusts of over 100MPH can be expected, fortunately in Winter. Many ordinary plants just won't grow. Herbacious plants, dormant in Winter and fast-growing in the short season are often best. Late flowering plants are out, but alpines thrive. The only Winter-standing vegetables that remain edible are kale and leeks, and even they are getting pretty mashed by January.

Windbreaks are essential. We set a row of slabs, and planted currant bushes behind them. Now the young brassicas are not blown out of the ground, or the tatties mashed down, by a Summer gale. Brassicas seem hardly worth the strug-

gle though. If the young plants aren't ruined by wind, or eaten by leatherjackets, cabbage rootfly or slugs then many a happy hour has to be spent removing the cabbage white eggs (and later caterpillars) from the leaves. The cabbages invariably bolt, the sprouts can be very thin but there usually is a nice crop of broccoli and some cauliflowers. One year, however a rat invaded from the farm – it ate the broccoli, and gnawed at the tatties. I wondered why the cauliflowers were taking so long to flower – and discovered that every single flower-head been eaten off when small.

Pests are however less severe than in a warm climate. It's too cold for wasps or ants and usually too breezy for midges. Most weeds are also less vigorous, even ground-elder can be vanquished. Buttercup and thistle however would take over if given half a chance.

Frost is less of a problem on a hill (cold air pools and valleys are colder on frosty nights) so fruit bushes do well unless the flowers are blown off in a gale as happens every other year. It's a real a treat to eat home-grown currants and gooseberries from the freezer in January. Everything ripens months later than the books say. Strawberries, gooseberries and currants in late July or August, raspberries in September. We're still often picking peas and broad beans in October, if the crop hasn't failed in a cold wet Summer or a storm hasn't finished them off.

Peas – the long days of June mean that 'dwarf' (45 centimetre) peas grow to a height of well over a metre. Every Spring I erect a fence, posts, wire mesh and all, to support them, you can forget the few sticks recommended by the books!

As bushes, flowers and general lushness have increased so the birds have moved in, chaffinches, green-finches, thrushes, robins. It is strange to hear blackbirds calling while snipe are drumming overhead, the garden is a lush oasis in open fields leading onto moorland. A phenomenal number of bumblebees visit the flowers and shrubs, and there's nothing better than sitting out on a brilliant Caithness afternoon looking across to those distant mountains and listening to the bees buzzing on the fuschia.

No doubt if it hadn't been for the garden I'd have finished off the Munros long ago. The creation of a garden amid miles of bare fields and moor, 400 feet up on the north coast of Scotland is certainly just as much of a challenge!

Triathlon!

The Wick Triathlon? Just a doddle, I thought. Three miles run – only a lunch-time jog. Twelve miles cycle – less than a one way journey to work. 750 metres swim – well, a bit tougher, that, but only 25 minutes of swimming up and down the pool. So when I saw it advertised for the end of August, a fun entry seemed in order.

When the day came the family needed the car, so I had to cycle across to Wick. With such an easy day ahead I wasn't too bothered, it wouldn't be an onerous 20 miles on a mild, quiet morning, I conserved my energy by just pottering along the lanes through Gillock, taking over an hour and a half for the ride.

On arrival at the Wick swimming pool, misgivings rapidly started to grow. Everyone turning up seemed to be half if not a third of my age, all were dressed for the part and looked extremely fit. Bad memories of school sports started coming back, of collapsing with a stitch before completing one circuit of a 440 yard track, of being unable to swim one length of the pool... Competitive sports have never been my thing. Never had I 'raced' over three miles running or 12 miles cycling and certainly not 30 lengths swimming, now I was faced with all three at once.

I'd put down a time of 25 minutes for the 30 lengths, reckoning this was pretty fast if I went flat out. The list of times expected by others came as a bit of a shock, most were under 15 minutes and some were under ten. At least I was in a lane with other slow-coaches. I was strongly tempted to get back on the bike and quietly disappear off to Dunbeath or somewhere on what was now turning into a very nice day. But I'd paid my £8 entry fee and been thoroughly marked with my number, in indelible pen, on my arms and legs. It was too late to back out.

I'd always wondered how triathlons were organised. The bikes are placed in a long row in a rack, with space next to them to put your cycling and running things. This is known as 'the transition area'. The pool changing room is available for a quick change from swimming trunks to shorts and T-shirt, though many just leap on the bike in their trunks or wet shorts and set off, bare feet in cycle shoes, After six miles out to Bilbster and back you leave the bike, change into running shoes (if you wish) and set off for three laps round Pultneytown. (again bad memories of getting lost on school cross country 'runs' when I'd invariably come in last. Once a search party was sent out..)

There were about 80 people taking part, and since you couldn't have more than about 20 swimming at once, four heats. Three or four people swam in each lane of the pool. I was in the second heat and so watched the first with interest. The good swimmers 'crawled' up and down the pool at incredible speed with fancy diving turns at the end of the lengths. Others, were slower, with breast stroke. Nobody had ever shown me how to do this properly or how to turn so I watched carefully – perhaps a bit late to learn now! Before the second heat could start everyone from the first batch had to finish so we all watched the last person swimming up and down an otherwise empty pool. That would be me when my turn came…

Now our turn to get in the water. We're off!. Surprisingly, going flat out, I could just keep up with the other three in my lane. Why are they stopping after two lengths? Sorry, this is just a warm-up. The real start is not till ten shivering minutes later.

I can swim 30 or 40 lengths, slowly, without too much trouble but had never tried going fast over that distance. As expected the other three soon drew ahead of me, then caught up behind, the rule is that you let people past at the end of a length if they grab your foot. I'd forgotten to bring my goggles and my eyes were getting sore. Attempts at fast turns worked once or twice but more often wasted time and left me trying to breathe water. Basically I was flailing about and wasting energy while others coasted along easily at about twice my speed. Then, as expected, I was the last in the pool, all eyes on my own peculiar version of breast stroke.

Eventually my 30 lengths were complete, in about 24 minutes, and I hauled myself out to cheers (jeers?) and staggered into the changing room feeling shattered. No time to get dry, just pull on shorts, socks, T-shirt and stumble out to the bike. There was a mist outside – or was it my eyes? It was my eyes. For the next few miles on the bike they streamed with water. Cycling is another 'sport' where I can cover the distance but have no speed. I just had to try and not be 'lapped' by the next heat who would already be half-way through the swim. A slight following wind helped, I just pedalled as hard as I could, and very gradually gained ground on someone ahead. Already the faster people in my heat were heading back into to Wick, though at least some seemed to be suffering a little. Turn round at Bilbster Bridge, back along the same road, now meeting people hurtling out towards me. Pushing really hard I was catching up the man in front – just managed to pass – and it was a woman. Cycle racing looks easy but even 12 miles is really tough (at least that's how I find it), something like the 'Tour de France' is just ten grades of complete impossibility .

At last back to the pool, leave the bike, change into running shoes and off again. The running was for me the easiest, I'd given up trying to go fast and just jogged along at a snail's pace. Young marshals were out on all the corners showing the way so there was no risk of getting lost, the route led down to the harbour then steeply up Harbour terrace, along Breadalbane Terrace, past the Assembly Rooms and the Groat offices then back along the river, three times round. It was now Sunday afternoon and all the town was quiet. The best thing about the route was passing the hospital where I'd spent a short spell ten months earlier; they looked after me well and did a good job for me to be fit enough again to be running the triathlon!

Eventually, in what turned out to be fifth from last position, behind all the Wick Ladies Joggers and the teenagers, I finished. A great event, superb organisation, friendly atmosphere, lovely spread of food laid on for the finishers, And a really nice T-shirt to go with it. If I can manage it, anyone can – have a go next year!

There was still the matter of cycling home. But with a good following wind down the Castletown road in the hot sun, this turned out to be the most enjoyable part of the day, just pedal gently, stop to look at the flowers, no hurry!

Could I now call myself an iron man? NO! The REAL triathlon, the so-called 'iron man' is about TEN times as much: three-mile swim, 120 miles cycle and 26-mile run. I think I'll give that one a miss. But if I wear my 'Wick Triathlon' T-shirt when I'm down south, no-one will know.

Day return to Rousay

It's easy to forget about Orkney. Oh yes, we know its there, like China, a long way off and visited about as often. But we all should, from time to time, join the tourists for a little trip over the water to those friendly green and brown isles.

So a fine but misty morning saw me pedalling off to John O' Groats for the 9AM Pentland Venture sailing. It was to be a long day of boats and hills, of sun and wind, of hard pedalling and quiet sitting at sunny piers.

Mist began thickening to fog and the south-east wind was picking up, but at the pier the sun was shining and fog was only clinging to Duncansby Head. Ticket bought, I sat back to await the first boat of the day. Rough or smooth, I always enjoy the crossing to Orkney, the secret being to dress warmly and stay on deck! This crossing was calm, but misty, with nothing to see from the middle of the Firth till the cliffs of South Ronaldsay hove into sight.

Everyone else boarded three buses for Kirkwall which roared past after a mile or so, leaving me pedalling north on my own. The weather slowly brightened and cleared, the sun grew hotter, the wind was mostly from behind. Heather and scabious brightened the roadside verges, sea glittered on one side, the other side, or both. Friendly farms, crofts and little villages passed, what more can a cyclist ask for!

The 'Italian Chapel' on Lamb Holm is usually only seen in the company of about three busloads of people (and is worth visiting even then). This morning I had the place to myself; very peaceful and more miraculous than ever. The visitors' book held more than 4000 signatures in August alone.

Kirkwall is not my favourite town but is redeemed by St Magnus Cathedral. Well I remember doing the 80-mile round trip by bike and ferry on a Sunday to visit the cathedral and finding it shut! A visit always leaves one refreshed – my particular favourites being the great Norman columns and the new West window – though Caithnessians find its portrayal of the Flotta flare (and all the oil-based pollution it symbolises) rather odd.

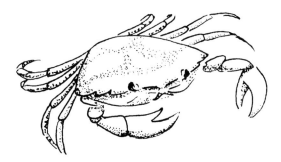

The main Kirkwall-Finstown road is Orkney's nearest thing to a motorway and a good route to miss on the bike. Instead I pedalled up the quiet alternative road climbing over the southern side of Wideford Hill. A chambered cairn, among heather overlooking the bay, gave a good sunny spot for lunch. A torch had been left there for the use of visitors exploring the 5000-year-old interior chambers.

Next destination was the 2PM Rousay ferry from Tingwall, seven miles north. Time was short and I hammered along the endless straights, arriving with ten minutes to spare to discover that the ferry actually went at 2.30. Time for a quick dip in the sea.

I'd never, to my shame, visited Rousay and now had just over two hours to explore it. The island is dominated by moorland hills rising to over 800 feet, with good farmland around the coast, many antiquities and all in all is a delightful place.

I followed the hilly single-track road which circuits the island in about 15 miles, through heather and small fields in the afternoon sun. A long steep climb took me to the north-east corner from where the road cut diagonally down across the steep northern slopes dropping into the sea. Leaving the bike I climbed up to one of the higher tops for a view over the interior of the island, mostly moorland with a loch right in the middle. The wind was rising and it was slow, hard work pedalling on round into a strong south-easterly.

Two 5500-year-old cairns gave cause for stopping; one long and divided into chambers by huge stones and the other a remarkable two-storey structure. Man had lived here a long time. The views over the shining sea to Eynhallow and Mainland were magnificent but marred by the huge (not even working) windmills on Burgar Hill opposite – whatever one's views on wind-power nobody could call those particular structures anything other than ugly and totally out of place. They have since been dismantled and replaced with more graceful designs.

After the hard ride it was nice to sit back in the hot sun on the boat for the 20-inute return crossing to Tingwall.

There remained another 15 miles or so to ride, across the hills to Stenness and on to Stromness. The steep climb up to the 'Chair of Lyde', Orkney Mainland's nearest thing to a hill pass, had me walking at this stage of the day, but gave in compensation a lovely downhill run through miles of heather to the green fields of Western Mainland.

Here I had to turn straight into the wind which, funnelling over the hills further south had increased to near gale-force. The 'St.Ola' wasn't going to wait for me, there was nothing for it put to push really hard. Getting past Maeshowe was a struggle but then, with the wind from the side, the miles passed quickly till Stromness appeared below, evening sun on its grey roofs and walls, with the hazy hills of Hoy beyond. There was plenty of time after all and once again I found myself sitting at a harbour in the sunshine waiting for the boat.

Surprisingly, the sea was nearly calm and the crossing back to Scrabster almost like a cruise. A warm wind, scented of heather, blew down from the high cliffs of Hoy as the sun set. Dusk fell, the moon rose, Dunnet Head lighthouse flashed in the distance and the lights of Thurso gradually drew nearer. All that remained was a seven mile cycle home from Scrabster in the warm Summer-scented dark, the Aurora Borealis glowing faintly to the north. The trip to Rousay had been a long day but well worth the effort.

An amble on Hoy

Four-thirty on a Monday morning. Pitch dark, rising wind and rain hammering on the windows. The thought of going back to bed was very tempting but the weather might be worse a week later! So, at five I set off to pedal down to Scrabster. Miraculously, the rain had stopped, the wind had eased, and the sky was lightening.

Almost every day I see across to the tremendous cliffs and high rolling hills of Hoy, only 15 miles away. Hoy has not, however, been an easy place to reach, demanding two nights away from home just to spend one good day on the island. New sailing times of the 'St Ola' had changed things and a day return, with more than just two or three hours on Hoy, became possible. Only on a Monday, before the end of October, could it be done by catching the 6AM boat from Scrabster and returning on the 8PM from Stromness.

So, with a day's leave from work booked I was on my way. Remember the 5.30AM train? Thurso dark and dead, with the only life the lighted train in the station. The feeling was just the same as I pedalled through the deserted town and down the hill to Scrabster, where a few fishermen were getting ready for a dawn sailing and a few cars were lined up for the boat. It was strange to go into the P & O office at such an early hour to buy a ticket from a bright and efficient lady at the desk.

Even the short sailing to Orkney always has a feeling of adventure about it. More than usual, this time, as the boat pulled out into the dawn light and headed towards the cliffs of Hoy, where I hoped to be standing seven hours later.

If you've never been across, a trip on the Ola is a must – but choose a reasonably calm day unless you are a good sailor! The new Ola is much better but the old Ola was never the most comfortable of boats and had a somewhat queasy motion which became steadily worse as the sea roughened. I always stay in the fresh air on deck, however cold it is and in any case there is so much to see.

Not being a seafarer I find the view of Thurso from the bay fascinating, as the cliffs of Holburn Head recede into the distance. It is surprising how prominent Olrig hill, with its masts, becomes. But it is the cliffs of Hoy that draw the eye, slowly growing in stature as the boat approaches, till you realise how immense they really are.

A clearance was coming in from the west and the wind was rising to near gale; with the binoculars I could see the waterfalls blowing backwards up the Hoy cliffs near the Sneuk. The views of the Old Man of Hoy and the 1200-foot cliffs of St John's Head are tremendous from the boat, if you're feeling well enough to look! Fortunately the sea was not yet too rough, and I just felt a bit queasy. It was going to be a boisterous day.

We came into Stromness with the swell, the wind from behind. Surely that first view of Stromness from the sea is one of the best of Orkney sights, with the line of higgeldy-piggeldy stone houses along the shore, each with its own slipway.

Only eight and already in Stromness! The Hoy boat left at 8.30; just time for a brief wander along the cobbled street where it was only another Monday morning for those going to work.

There were only a few passengers on the little 'Jessie Ellen'; the lady schoolteacher who sat in the cabin with the captain and his lad, a man with briefcase and pullover who read a book for the whole crossing and a few day-trippers like myself. The boat pulled out of the harbour and rounded Graemsay to the west, passing below the low cliffs and lighthouse in a decidedly choppy sea. A wartime ship, half sunk, blocks the channel and must be circumvented; the decks were partly grass grown and dozens of cormorants and shags lined the rusting railings.

Soon we were tied up at the Moaness pier, on North Hoy. There is now a ro-ro sailing to Lyness from Houton, but the boat from Stromness is still the best way onto Hoy. The school-bus was there, waiting for the teacher; I immediately set off walking along the shore. It was only nine in the morning and there were a whole seven and a half hours to spend on the island before the return sailing.

With its high rolling hills, tremendous cliffs, and difficulty of access, North Hoy is a magic place. In the time between ferries you either potter across to look at the Old Man or race to cover as much ground as possible. I chose the latter option; having made such an effort to get there I wasn't wasting time!

First, along the coast in warm morning sun, 50 curious seal heads watching from the water. The next imperative – the Dwarfie Stane, a huge boulder below sombre broken crags out of which a tomb was hollowed 5000 years ago and closed off by another huge boulder which now lies fallen beside the entrance.

Above the stone I scrambled up beside the crags through very rough slippery tussocks and long heather – there are no deer and few sheep to keep the growth down. Soon I reached the bare, rolling hilltops which give much better walking across gale-blasted stones and stunted vegetation. I headed south, across the 1310-foot 'Knap of Trowieglen' hoping to have time to reach the 600-foot cliffs at the strange in name, and appearance, 'Candle of the Sneuk'.

A south-westerly gale was blowing, but the sky was bright and the air clear. It is always strange to see a familiar view from the other direction, with Dunnet Head and the long north coast of the mainland to the south and the friendly huddle of buildings at Dounreay just visible 30 miles away. East was the huge Flotta oil terminal, with all the isles of Scapa Flow, and north the Orkney Mainland.

Great skuas, ever present on the Hoy Hills, circled and a pair dive-bombed in a half-hearted manner. The breeding season was over which was as well; angry great skuas with nests are not to be treated lightly. Great heavy birds, they come straight at you, silently, undeterred by shouts or waving arms and (usually) just miss your head. Arctic hares are another feature of the Hoy hills, and I must have seen half a dozen during the course of the day's walk. Also present on the hill lochans are divers, both black and red throated, and I saw (and heard the weird wailing of) a pair of each.

Tide and ferries wait for no man. I wanted to see Rackwick Bay, the Old Man and the high cliffs and alas there was just not time to get to the Sneuk. I'd see it another time. Still hurrying I took a ridge west of the disappointing boggy hollow which the map intriguingly named 'The Summer of Hoy'. The wind howled across the top of the great 600-foot sandstone cliffs east of Rackwick, here a few sheep tracks gave better going but the sheep had more nerve than me in the way they wandered round the tops of vertical-sided geos.

Now Rackwick bay was below, with just a steep 500-foot descent needed to reach the breaking waves. Sun shone, waves rolled in and smashed on the huge rounded boulders which make up this mile long bay. It is a pebble-beach for giants. A grand spot to eat lunch, in the salt spray and sun, always my favourite spot on Hoy – and there, out at sea was the sturdy Ola, heading north on its third crossing of the day.

A few warmly dressed but scantily shod people were on the shore – and there was a coach parked! Times have certainly changed, even on Hoy. An elderly couple were attempting the slippery path climbing up towards the Old Man, the woman hauling herself along the fence to get round a boggy patch. It is, how-

ever, a good two miles rough walk to the Old Man from Rackwick along a path which has now become one of those five-metre wide eroded bogs more characteristic of the Pennines.

Tide and ferries wait for no man. I had just over three hours to do the whole walk along the western cliffs of Hoy, a walk which one could take a day over. I knew what the going would be like, having done it a couple of times before, and reckoned that by pushing hard it was just possible.

Ahead, a man in his early 60s was striding out through the bogs. I overtook, apologising for my rush. This, the least interesting stretch, was the best to hurry over. A hazard of walking alone is that of meeting the occasional gregarious walker who for some reason, has been forced to walk without company. When he or she says 'Mind if I join you?' there is little you can do – you don't know their experience, state of fitness, capabilities, inclinations – and if they insist on sticking with you, you are saddled with a responsibility that can ruin the walk.

It transpired that the man I passed was also making for the ferry, and had intended to return to Rackwick and take the quick path back across the island. When he heard that I was taking another route he evidently decided to follow. He was still only a few yards behind when the 'Old Man' came into view. I stopped for a quick bite to eat at the cliff-edge, admiring the scene and watching the breaking waves with some concern for the return crossing to Scrabster that night. He stopped too and yes, he was going to follow me. I hoped he was fit. If he tired suddenly, or sprained an ankle in the rough country we'd have to cross, his safety would now be MY responsibility...

Fortunately he WAS fit, though I felt sorry for him at being forced through such tremendous country at such a pace. From the Old Man a narrow, wet path climbs north for two miles. All the time the cliffs to the west grow higher, till you are standing next to a vertical 1200 foot drop into the sea. The scale is only appreciated if a boat is sailing past below. The highest point, St Johns Head, is a flat acre ringed by these immense cliffs and can be reached by an easy scramble. I have done it but there is a drop of 1000 feet to the side and I must have had more nerve in the past!

Now we turned east, crossing the rough moor to Su Fea and then down across a long bare stony saddle to reach the big cairn on the second highest of Hoy hills, Cuilags. This overlooks Moaness with Stromness just four miles away – and there was the Ola again, just heading out into Hoy Sound on its fourth crossing. A big swell was now coming in and I could see the bow dipping into the waves and the spray flying. We picked our way slowly down steep slopes to the

glen, with just an easy two-mile walk remaining to the ferry and a very choppy crossing back to Stromness.

With a couple of hours to spare before the Ola sailed, I bought a chip supper (later to be regretted) and wandered up to the top of Brinkies Brae, the little hill above the town, to eat it. Scapa Flow was spread out beyond the grey houses of Stromness, with the high Hoy hills beyond. North rolled the bare fields, stone walls and lochs of the mainland.

There was something moving, on the horizon. Far away, a great white arm was ponderously lifting itself up above the hills and going down again, once every second. It was the huge windmill on Burgar Hill, over 12 miles away and unavoidably catching the eye even at that distance.

Just after 8PM the Ola set off for its sixth crossing (imagine 180 miles across the Pentland Firth in one day!) It was now cold and clear, south-west wind perhaps force six or seven, swell out at sea maybe 20–30 feet. Pretty calm conditions compared to those often experienced, but still the roughest I'd been across in, with the decks tilting at angles which certainly looked and felt like 30 degrees. By the time we were past Hoy I had reached the stage of fixing my eyes on the distant lights of Thurso as a steady reference point and holding on tight…

At last, suddenly, there was the welcome smell of land and we were in calm water off Holburn Head. Teeth chattering and cold to the bone (my fault, I didn't HAVE to stay on deck!) I alighted, recovered the bike from where I'd chained it by the cattle pens and wobbled off homewards. After a few miles I'd warmed up and felt better – and was in the door at 11.15PM, over 18 hours after setting out that morning.

Fair Isle

'Fancy a trip to Fair Isle tomorrow morning?' It isn't a question you quite expect on a Saturday evening. A friend whose hobby was flying planned to make the trip on Sunday morning, there would be an hour or two on the island before returning around lunch time. He had an empty seat…

It was, indeed, one of the very few days in the year when such a trip was possible in a light, single-engined plane. The weather was almost totally calm, as well as being very clear with just broken cloud at around 4000 feet. So, very early on a September Sunday morning I was cycling across bumpy fields near Halkirk in search of a little plane. I found it parked at the corner of one of the larger fields, one which didn't have cows in it. This was the airport; a ruined croft served as the terminal building with a strip of polythene on a post as a windsock.

Shortly after 7.30 we bumped across the grass into the air, flew low over Halkirk and climbed up over Olrig Hill and Dunnet Head. The distance was about 100 miles, the route being over as much land as possible so that, in the (unlikely) event of failure of the single engine an emergency landing would be possible. Still, we wore life-jackets, just in case…

A year later in fact the same pilot and plane had to make an emergency landing in the Great Glen when the engine lost power. Quite an epic, dodging low power lines and fences and trees and coming to rest a few feet from the shore of Loch Lochy. ('I'm not doing that again!', he said, when I mentioned Fair Isle…)

Stroma passed below, then over the Pentland Firth to South Ronaldsay and up to Kirkwall which we crossed just 20 minutes after leaving Halkirk. I'd never seen Orkney from the air and the next part of the flight, over the small isles from Shapinsay across Eday and Sanday to North Ronaldsay was fascinating. Fertile green fields rising like irregular jigsaw pieces from the sea, the Northern Orkneys looked like the remaining high ground of a landscape which had been inundated by sea – which of course it is.

From the air I could see the stone wall around North Ronaldsay, built to keep the seaweed-eating sheep on the shore (and out of the fields), then we passed over the lighthouse and could see, still 25 miles off, a low, dark island – our destination.

Briefly we climbed up through the cloud into bright sunshine then descended through another gap as we neared Fair Isle. I could see now that the island was anything but flat, just a little larger than Stroma, and with high cliffs on its western side. We circled the island, descending, flying over the white crofts on the southern, populated part, over the harbour, over the high northern cliffs, before coming in low for a perfect landing on the gravelly airstrip.

It was not yet nine (Were you still in bed?!). Just one short morning to explore an island I'd never been to before, and hadn't even studied in a map! I set off jogging, determined to see as much as possible.

First I headed north for the highest point of the island, Ward Hill, over seven hundred feet high. The scenery up there and along the clifftops is very like parts of the north coast of Sutherland, for instance between Strathy and Bettyhill. The ground is covered with short grass and heather, with dramatic cliffs and geos falling into the sea. Sharp and clear to the north were the hills of Shetland, 25–40 miles away with further west the hilly isle of Foula. Far to the south, Orkney was visible and all around the sea, glittering as the cloud began to break into warm September sunshine.

I followed the clifftops for a mile southwards, back towards the airstrip and cut across back to the plane. Two children arrived on bikes for a look, I found their accent hard to understand and when I told them I'd come from Caithness that morning got the reply 'Where's Caithness?' There is a primary school on the island but secondary age children board in Lerwick.

Fair Isle is a mecca for birdwatchers, particularly in Autumn when rare migrants pass through giving 'twitchers' an opportunity to add to their list of sightings. There is an observatory and hostel; by now those staying were up and about and people with binoculars, telescopes and cameras kept appearing on skylines and clifftops. The sixty or so residents on the island would be mostly going to church.

Now I jogged south, down the road through the white crofts, passing the occasional birdwatcher. This part of the island is dominated by a large windmill which supplies electricity – when the wind is blowing and not too strong – a generator was throbbing instead in the windless conditions. Fields were mostly grass grazed by sheep and a few cows, with the odd patch of (green) oats.

I carried on up to the top of the 500-foot cliffs near the southern tip of the island; here was a coastguard lookout hut and a magnificent view over shimmering sea to distant islands. Then back north again, round a 'gloup' resembling that on Stroma, across the airstrip and down to the island's main harbour. A cargo boat, rather smaller than the 'Pentland Venture', makes twice weekly crossings to Shetland. The boat was hauled out of the water, a couple of notches on the propeller testifying to rough crossings.

In the last half-hour I wandered up to the grassy top of the cliffs opposite the 'sheep rock'. This dramatic 500-foot sea-stack is joined to the island by a narrow arete and has an outline that characterises Fair Isle from afar. It was lovely just to sit in the warm sun for a while and look around after running about 12 miles around the island!

Shortly after noon we were airborne again, circling the island then heading south, back across the green North Orkney Isles, now basking in sunshine. We flew in over Caithness at about 1000 feet, crossing my house so that the family could come out to wave, and then over Halkirk for a bumpy landing on the field.

As I cycled homewards, shortly after two, there was still time left for an afternoon in the garden. And what did you do, that Sunday morning?

Strathy Point coast

The proposal for a Caithness coastal path, from Helmsdale to Melvich, leaves me with mixed feelings. There is no doubt that the Caithness coastal scenery is magnificent, some of the best in Britain. It is surely selfish to keep it to ourselves and a coastal path would encourage many others to discover the beauties of the county. However there are seal colonies, peregrine nesting sites, puffin stacks and so on which could be spoilt by too much disturbance.

The walk around the coast is already possible without a long distance path but it is perhaps elitist to suggest that anyone can walk it now; most simply won't go without an official, designated route.

A long distance route is always walked at a speed of miles per hour in order to get through, for example, 100 miles of Caithness coast in a reasonable time such as a week. There will be no choice but to miss out most of the headlands and take shortcuts between the ends of the geos. To explore the coast properly, you have to progress instead at a speed of hours per mile! It has taken me over 15 years to explore the whole coast from Helmsdale to Eribol.

I walked from Armadale to Strathy point on a recent Saturday and it took five hours, without dawdling, to cover three or four map miles from the beach to the point.

Expecting a day of squalls and gales I was pleasantly surprised when the early lashing showers abated and the day turned into one of sunshine and a moderating westerly wind. I strode out across the empty beach (often empty even on fine Bank Holidays) and set of along what initially appears a less interesting stretch of coast to the east.

But there is always so much to see! First a deep gloup, then a headland with an old fort on a stack – quite a scramble up and down. There are several little stony beaches below Aultiphurst (Have you ever driven down those roads signposted Brawl, Aultiphurst, Fleuchary, between Melvich and Strathy?) Near

Brawl is the Glupie Bhrawl; a narrow gloup connected to the sea by an arch over which you can scramble and with a superb blowhole, set in the side of the cliff, snorting away and emitting clouds of spray like steam. On, up over the headland of Cnoc Glas, cold in the fresh Westerly, now with increasingly fine scenery of cliff and stack and breaking wave.

While climbing up the next headland, opposite the small conical Boursa Island, I noticed a fine stony beach below – was there a way onto it? I retreated and discovered a steep scramble down, complete with a fixed rope as a handrail. At the bottom an old rusting winch was set into the stones – incredibly this beach, surrounded by rocks and skerries and with only one narrow channel out past the island, was used as a base for fishing. There are others like it, a tribute to the desperation of the StrathNaver folk evicted here. Strathy Point was considered one of the worst spots, exposed to all winds with no shelter at all.

When the tide is well out it is possible to get along below the cliffs for a quarter of a mile and scramble up by a waterfall on the other side of the headland – this time I managed most of the way but was turned back by the sea and had to go all the way back, up and round. After half an hour I was about 100 yards further along the coast; typical progress on these contorted cliffs!

It goes without saying that care is needed on clifftops but on the next stretch you really must watch out. The cliffs twist and turn at such a rate you can suddenly find yourself most unexpectedly on the edge of sheer drops and overhangs to black geos, looking down on stacks and breaking waves.

There is a steep slide down to the burn of Allt a Mhuillinn which you can follow, partly IN the burn as the only way, down to another fine stony beach. Then climb all the way back up again to an old lichened cairn above the crofts, on north to the smooth green grass of Rubha Meil Cuilce and back round another long deep geo which suddenly opens out below your feet.

The next section was simply magnificent, cliff scenery as good as any this side of Tongue. Deep geos, stacks, fulmars circling in clouds like snowflakes. Near is another once-fortified little grassy headland reached by a narrow neck between two geos, one of which was again once used as a harbour.

The best of the scenery was now past but on a fine clear day Strathy Point is always a grand place to be with airy views stretching from Dunnet Head to Hoy to Cape Wrath to the snowy peaks of Sutherland. I wandered out to the point, admiring the two model lighthouses set in the lighthouse loch, and then made my way slowly back across the moors to Brawl and Fleuchary.

Yet perhaps the best part of the day was kept till last. The tide was out and the low sun was gleaming on the white breakers and the wet sands of Armadale Bay. Spray drifted like thin mist above the empty beach in a scene of great beauty; there is hope yet for the world. Incredibly nobody else had been on the beach all day, the only footprints were my own. A coastal path which encouraged a few others to come and see might not be such a bad idea after all.

Sutherland in October

What takes you out now, season's turn,
To sodden moor and swollen burn?
To sandblast rain and shotblast hail,
To soaking sleet and force ten gale?

The stags, with straggling harems keep,
With barks and roaring, you from sleep,
As in your flimsy tent you lie,
Neath Valkyrie infested sky!

The salmon jumping up the fall,
Are heading homeward after all.
The croaking ptarmigan – its flocks,
Are home amongst the highest rocks.

The grey seal mothers in the geo,
Keep pups from reach of swash and flow,
Of storm waves – hills of smashing spray,
What brings you here on such a day?

Is life not more than work each day,
Of routine, of the 'normal' way,
Of weekend sleep, TV and shops,
Church, Sunday papers, household jobs?

What takes me out now, season's turn –
Why, sodden moor and swollen burn!
Tis God that speaks in sleet and hail,
His peace that rides the mountain gale!

Autumn gold

The roaring of the red-deer stags in rut conjures up Autumn in the Highlands more than almost anything else. It is a sound few however hear, unless they live in, or venture into, the hills. You don't have to go far though in Caithness to reach stag country.

Without even walking one step you can hear the animals. Just drive out to Shurrery Loch, or to the highest point of the road from Dunbeath to Braemor, on a calm dusk or early morning in the Autumn. Stop and just listen; you will hear the challenges roared back and forth, a great sound indeed.

Travelling from Caithness to any other part of the world just reminds us what a special place we live in. The Highlands, and Caithness, are truly unique. Living here, we tend to get blase about the scenery and the wildlife of the Highlands which stand comparison with the best anywhere in the world, and deserve much more esteem than they usually get.

Nowadays there is a tendency to dwell on evils of the past, clan warfare, clearances, deforestation, misuse of land. Few places on this globe have however escaped such things. Here and now, and in the future, there is more going for the North than almost anywhere else.

An early morning visit to Scaraben is a favourite Autumn outing of mine. Just 30 minutes drive took me from the rural farmland of north-east Caithness to the moorland above Braemor, the stags roaring in the dawn twilight, a light frost on the heather.

Ten minutes jog and a steep descent brought me to a shaky suspension bridge where the Berriedale Water flows though a short gorge, surely Neil Gunn had this spot in mind when he wrote his 'Well at the World's End'. Then it was steeply up, through heather at first, onto the bare, wind-blasted Scaraben ridge. You'd need to go nearly 2000 feet higher in the Cairngorms to encounter similar terrain. There is always a cold wind and usually at least a gale.

From all sides came the sound of the stags, they took little notice of me, more concerned with each other and their hinds. Much is made of the difficulty of stalking but in my experience it is often difficult NOT to get close to the animals.

Stony slopes led to the eastern, subsidiary top, then another half-mile, down and up, to the main top. Below to the left, where the steep slopes run out onto heather moor, a fence surrounds a spring from where the 'Caithness Spring' water was piped for the two miles to the Berriedale bottling plant. 'Bottled from a pure spring on the side of Mount Scara', said the labels. Really! Since when had we heard of Mount Nevis?

Early on a clear Autumn morning, the top of Scaraben is a fine place from which to appreciate the beauties and contrasts of the far North. Westwards stretch miles of empty yellow and red moor and mountain, true wilderness, whatever the fashionable critics may say. Most of it was never inhabited, even before the clearances. The woods and greenery of Berriedale are a sharp contrast, with the Berriedale windmill turning and beyond, out at sea, the oil rigs of the Beatrice Field. Eastwards, the miles of grey coast, north across the flow country to the fertile farmland of north-east Caithness and beyond the hills of Orkney. At least half a dozen very different worlds in the space of 360 degrees.

The air warmed rapidly in the sun as I jogged back down, the stags now quieter. The Berriedale valley would be a famous 'beauty spot' elsewhere, here it's just one of hundreds of similar. The place one is NOW is always the best, and that morning there was nowhere better to be than the bridge over the brown waters thundering through the gorge in the Autumn sunshine.

A roundabout route, via old settlements and sheepfolds, took me back to the Braemore road and the car. The morning had still hardly begun, so there was

plenty of time for a detour on the way home. A gentle walk along the track from Dunbeath took me to the 'Prisoners Leap'. It was years since I'd last visited this spot (when did you last go there?) and I'd forgotten just how spectacular it is. The Dunbeath Water runs through a narrow gorge between 50-foot crags from where (with care!) you can look straight down into the peaty water. Would a leap across have been possible? I very much doubt it.

Again it's one of those spots that would be famous in other countries, with at the very least a visitor centre or gift shop. God forbid that we do likewise here but it goes to show that such magnificent scenery is simply commonplace in this part of the world. Tourists who stay here are usually bowled over by the area and a little more discrete encouragement of them can do no harm. The Scottish Highlands, and Caithness in particular, really is one of the finest places in the world!

Planes and cars and bikes and trains

Flying takes you so abruptly from one environment to another. Just a few hours after cycling home on a quiet day of drizzle I found myself driving at 80MPH down the M62 (or was it the M61, or M56, or?) from Manchester airport in a hire car during the late evening rush hour. Streams of headlights, four lanes, cloverleafs, flyovers, just keep behind the car in front and hope for the best. Whatever was I doing here?

Barring fog, accidents, road works or just traffic jams, motorways are at least fast, and little more than an hour later I was suddenly into the quiet Dales village of Winton where my mother lives. She once pointed out that I always arrive by a different route or means of transport, and indeed in the years since she moved there I must by now have exhausted most of the possibilities.

To fit an extra day or two in Cumbria into a work trip south can be quite complicated. A December visit to Sellafield gave the chance to hire a car from Newcastle airport with, on the way across, a walk on the Weardale Fells for the first time in many years. That allowed two nights in Winton, with a drive to Sellafield via the 1 in 3 Lake District passes of Wrynose and Hard Knott. On another occasion after a meeting at Risley, near Liverpool, the Sellafield contingent gave me a lift north, letting me off near Tebay. It was February, dark, and raining – but I was prepared, changing from office to walking clothes and striding out along the disused railway through Smardale, over the 50-metre high viaduct, through dark wet woods, owls hooting, and by country lanes to reach Winton by eight.

Crossing the Pennines on foot used to be a favourite route of mine, by bus up Weardale then across the emptiest part of England, over Chapel fell to Teesdale then across Mickle Fell, Little Fell, and down through army ranges to Brough (pronounced Bruff, not Broch or Brow!) You aren't supposed to venture on these ranges when firing is in progress but with horses and sheep grazing I reckon the risk must be small. A grey November day with the mist right down and hoar frost building up on the tops would mean compass bearings for miles. Another, easier route was 20 miles over the moors from Barnard Castle,

Until Kirkby Stephen station, on the Settle-Carlisle line, reopened a few years ago, the nearest railway station to Winton was 10 miles away at Appleby. The walk from there to Winton was always pleasant, much of it along the river Eden, and was a good way of waking up after a night's travel. Usually I'd have caught the overnight train from Inverness to Glasgow which, alas, no longer runs. From Kirkby Stephen it is less than four miles to walk, but there was little way of avoiding a mile along a busy main road which could be horrendous in the dark. (There is now a footpath.)

Once, I caught the early morning flight from Wick down to Manchester for a day's meeting in Risley. The meeting over, a car took me to Warrington in time for the train up the west coast line to Penrith. There was no point carrying on to Carlisle, the last train south to Kirkby Stephen would have gone. But I'd studied the timetable and realised that there was just time to get a taxi for the four miles to Langwathby which would let me join the Carlisle-Settle train there.

Knowing Penrith station well, I was able to walk down the train so as to be immediately opposite the station entrance when the train stopped, and so first out of the station and into one of the only two taxis! All went well and I was in Winton before 8PM (two taxis, two planes, two official cars, a day's meeting, two trains and a four-mile walk after leaving home that morning). As a last resort I've twice had to take a taxi all the way from Penrith or Oxenholme, after arriving on a late train with absolutely no other means of transport (once coming from London, once coming from Edinburgh)

My first visit to Winton, after my parents moved there, was in the hard Winter of 1978. Bikes were easy to take on trains then and I'd cycled down to Thurso for the 5.30AM train, then out of Penrith some 13 hours later. The 25 miles to Winton should have been easy along the back roads but the bike was overladen and it was dark and icy. I remember pedalling gingerly through Appleby while the Salvation Army band played Christmas carols, and finally having to walk the last mile where the road was a sheet of ice. That visit ended by cycling off to the Lake District along a wonderfully empty A66 with Stainmore blocked by snow and no traffic getting through from the east.

Another frosty October night I cycled from Oxenholme on a new bike which I'd just bought in Waterloo while passing through London from France. At midnight I was hurtling down Ash Fell towards Kirkby Stephen, the icy air in my face a considerable contrast to the previous day's heat in Grenoble!

Then there was that February 1st when I caught the overnight train from Inverness to Preston, and set off on the bike at 4.45AM from Preston station on a 70 mile ride over the Forest of Bowland. It snowed, hard. The wind blew. But I made it, eventually, by lunchtime.

I've actually driven it from Caithness surprisingly few times, the 450 miles is quite feasible in a day but I'm not a devotee of long distance driving. The worst journey was when I had to drive through the night after a day at work, stopping at one point for 40 winks in a layby on the A9. A police car stopped to investigate – 'Having a snooze? That's fine!'

With a baby in the car, feed and nappy stops were necessary. Once with temperatures in the 90's, we'd taken the Trinafour road hoping for a cool stop at 1500 feet. No such thing, the lack of shelter and beating June sun made the heat even more overpowering. Another stop on that journey was cut short by an approaching thunderstorm on the Devil's Beef-Tub road.

So this trip ended as it began, down the motorway in the rush-hour to Manchester airport, a haven of peace in contrast to the seething traffic. I bought a zany book by Tom Holt which only compounded the feeling of total unreality which one gets when shuttling between rapid modes of transport. Elementary quantum mechanics, as everyone knows, tells us that we can't know, precisely, speed and position at the same time. Perhaps that was why when I'd actually at last stopped moving, I felt sort of smeared out over the M6, M62, various airports, planes, cars and taxis. If God had meant us to fly he'd have given us wings … one of these days I'll just have to walk the whole way.

Above the clouds

It is a truism that weather on the hills is different from weather in the valleys. How different is not always appreciated. Those who only climb high when the weather is fine will notice that it is cooler and windier on the tops, but that otherwise there is little difference. It is in poor weather that it is always worse, and sometimes incredibly worse, than low down.

After 30 years of hillwalking in all weathers it still often surprises me how a gentle wind and drizzle in the valley can be, on the summits, a hurricane where progress can only be made by crawling into a welter of stinging, lashing water. How warm sun can give way to an icy gale with a wind-chill factor of minus something incredible, into which you stagger over rock-hard ground which, you feel, has never thawed since the last ice-age.

A couple of weeks ago, after a spell of gales and rain, the wind swung round to the north and the temperature plummeted. The air was however wonderfully clear, with long views, and the high tops looked most enticing.

The wind was definitely chill at 1000 feet but the contrast when above 2000 feet was amazing. Only mid-October and a bitter gale, below freezing, as cold as the bitterest January day at sea-level in Caithness. Already the peat had frozen hard, rime had built up on the cairns and fence-posts. On the high pools foam had frozen and piled up at one side, like ice-flows. In spite of the sun it froze ever harder as the day went on. It was a day much more like mid-February than October.

A week later and much of the country was wrapped in grey, anticyclonic gloom. Fog and low cloud hung round, drizzle fell from time to time. On such a day a walk over the hills is a peaceful, grey, Autumnal experience and expecting such, I set off up a long valley in the early half-light. The cloud base was at around 1000 feet and after a few miles I climbed up into it, prepared for a long walk through quiet fog.

Just 800 feet higher up and the fog began to thin. The sun appeared, hazily, then ahead came a glimpse of the peak I was climbing, soaring clear up into blue sky. Just 200 feet more and I was out, above a sea of cotton wool cloud, peaks like islands rising all around.

Such an experience is akin to miracle, and rare indeed. The air was suddenly warm, a temperature inversion was keeping all the murk below the 2000-foot contour. Soon I'd stripped off to shorts; it was back to Summer!

It is indeed magical to be up on the hills on such a day when most of the population is enduring the gloom. However after a couple of hours I'd crossed all the peaks on my 'island'. I suppose the rest of the day could have been spent sunbathing, but just a couple of miles away rose a larger island of higher peaks. The trouble was, that in between lay a descent of 2000 feet and a similar climb back up again.

I reckoned that, in less than two hours I could be back into the sun – and plunged downwards into the fog. The damp cold enveloped me again and the compass was needed for the tricky descent through crags to the pass. Then I was out below the cloud, into the grey haze. Below was a motor road with tourist cars grinding up and down it.

A pleasant path would now give an alternative walk back through the hills, below the cloud base, to my starting point. The steep slopes leading up into the fog did not look inviting; it took faith to believe that the sun was shining up there! I girded up the loins and began the long steep pull up, soon to be surrounded again by the clammy fog.

I was beginning to wonder if the weather had changed, when again that faint trace of blue appeared, then the sun, and I climbed out of the mist onto the summit of the first peak. Only the very top 20 feet rose out of the cloud, the ridge carrying on to the next top dipped again into the mist before climbing out into glorious clear sunshine.

For the rest of that afternoon I pottered over the high tops, revelling in the unusual conditions and meeting a few other equally delighted walkers. Below the highest summit I dozed for 20 minutes in the warm late afternoon sun, the cloud a white sea stretching unbroken to the horizon, seemingly covering the whole world and all its sorrows. There can have been few other sunbathers that day in the whole of Britain, with the weather forecaster apologising for the pre-vailing gloom!

So, as the sun went down so did I, back, sadly, into the fog and out again below to a misty grey October dusk with the grass still wet from that morning's dew. Sometimes, miracles happen.

November Dales

The main western routes from Scotland to England have always been been con-
fined to a narrow strip of country between the Pennines and the Lake District; the
M6 and railway still go this way. Even the most hardened city dweller can hardly
fail to notice the scenery here on a fine day, but few of those dodging the motorway lorries or hurtling over Shap at 100MPH on the intercity expresses take time
to visit this delectable country south of the aptly named vale of Eden.

On the train between Penrith and Oxenholme I'm often to be found darting
from side to side of the carriage to catch nostalgic glimpses of old familiar haunts
and hills... but for once I had the opportunity to wander this country again on
foot for a few days .

November is a good time of year for the hills, provided one is prepared for
weather; the tourists have gone and the high country is itself again, peaceful and
beautiful whether cloaked in mist and driving rain or lit by low sun and dusted by
early snow.

Kirkby Stephen is a market town lying at the heart of this area – known by
many only as a refreshment stop on the main coach route from industrial North-
East England to Blackpool. On four successive days, I walked back to Kirkby,
having first obtained a lift out to various points of the compass.

I crossed the rolling grassy Howgill Fells from Sedbergh, hills familiar and
friendly from countless visits in heatwave and blizzard, dawn and moonlight,
thunderstorm and frost. A good walk in the North of England strikes a balance
between high hills and lower, rural country; my route continued through the
Autumn woods of Smardale and by field paths towards the lights of Kirkby Stephen
as darkness fell.

On a day of sharp frost I climbed up past frozen Sand Tarn to the millstone
grit scarps of Swarth Fell and Wild Boar Fell above Mallerstang and the famous
Settle-Carlisle railway. The rising, bitter wind gave cold weather for the shep-

herds who were whistling their dogs to round up the Swaledale sheep for the Autumn tupping.

From the rocky fringes of the Lake District I tramped for miles across the bare limestone hills bordering the Eden valley. High stone walls gave some shelter from the rattling showers which turned to continuous rain by Crosby Garrett. I walked the last few miles along lanes Autumn scented by leaves and cows, with the wind roaring in the trees as the wet day turned into a wild night.

On a day of snow, sleet, rain and cloud I circuited the high moors around the head of Swaledale to a summit where nine huge cairns, centuries old, stand overlooking Stainmoor. With dramatic suddenness the cloud blew clear revealing the Eden Vale mellow in the late afternoon sun. Above, the great cloud-capped bulk of the Cross Fell hills glowed red while Mickle Fell, freshly capped in snow, looked the remotest hill in England it is.

So a few days later as the train raced northwards up the Lune valley towards Shap, on the long journey from Liverpool to Thurso, it seemed more than ever that the snowy, sunlit fells above were old friends.

East coast storm

It definitely wasn't a day for the bike. Even the car couldn't get above 50 MPH on the road east, with a force nine gale bouncing the rain off the road in sheets, rain which held an increasing content of salt towards the east coast. When I stopped the car above Sarclet Bay I couldn't tell whether it was raining or not.

The wind, well above force ten at times, was funnelling up and over the cliff and doing its best to throw the entire North sea across the county. From the headlands and the geos clouds of white spray were blowing miles inland. A nice morning for a gentle saunter along the clifftops! Just getting out of the car without losing the doors proved tricky, and the storm was doing its best to rip gloves, waterproofs and rucksack out of my hands and send them hurtling back towards Thurso. Getting back into the car was a problem to be faced later.

The whole of the bay at Sarclet was white, huge waves rolling in and breaking across the stack to the north and through the gap between it and the cliffs. The flying water – whether fresh or salt made little difference – stung face and eyes. Truly spectacular weather. In such conditions it obviously isn't safe to go anywhere near the actual edge of the cliffs, even if it were possible to reach them. So keeping a little inland, I set off to stagger across the headland, keeping as near the sea as reasonably possible, aiming to follow the coast for the three miles down to Whaligoe.

This is one of the most interesting bits of the Caithness east coast, well worth exploring thoroughly on a fine Summer day. The cliff scenery is good with the usual stacks and geos, while just inland are the remains of many old crofts, as well as chambered cairns and brochs. The landscape is rocky, knobbly, heathery and very attractive on a day of brilliant blue northern skies and sun. This however was a day of rather different conditions. The huge waves were hitting the cliffs and more or less carrying on, with sheets of water blowing at me from the side, hammering on my cagoule like torrential rain. Streams of salt water ran down the slopes to the right into Loch Sarclet. Nobody was out sailing model yachts.

Beyond Loch Sarclet is the deserted farm of Ulbster Mains, with the cemetery and mausoleum. I crossed to the east, making my way up rough slopes to where a prominent plume of white spray was blowing inland. Ever so often a particularly big wave hitting the cliffs would send even more spray into the air, and white clouds of water would twist and writhe towards me, hose past and drive westward at 60MPH.

It turned out that the geos were generating much of the spray. Waves coming in and breaking in all directions were a turmoil of white water and the wind was simply lifting all the spray up and out over the end of the geo in a steady plume. There is a stack here which looks a bit like a horse, facing out to sea; it stood there, steady, as water boiled and steamed all around. Meanwhile the headland to the north looked like the bow of a ship with rough seas breaking across it.

A fence here marked the edge of cultivated land and I attempted to follow it eastwards. Wind was funnelling with particular force and I found myself hanging onto each fencepost and more or less making a run for the next. At the corner of the fence was an old metal strainer post, firmly fastened into rock; holding onto this against the wind was a bit like hanging off overhead bars. That proved the windiest spot. Apart from the rain and spray, and the usual difficulties of walking in a severe gale, progress was then a bit easier, up heather slopes to a little hilltop above a croft, then descending to round the end of Ellen's geo. The sea here was again a scene of indescribable chaos and confusion. Whaligoe would be interesting.

Local people were spending the morning well indoors, a couple of times I saw faces peering out of cottage windows, as from portholes of storm-tossed ships. At Whaligoe the analogy was even stronger. Seawater, whipped up from the neighbouring geo to the north, was hurtling over the top of the 200-foot cliffs and washing all the cottages like driving rain. Reaching the top of the steps proved difficult. I had no intention of going down, but fought my way to the first few to get a view down into the geo.

To my surprise the flight of steps was well sheltered from the worst of the storm and it was actually quite safe and easy to descend. It felt, however, like entering some witch's cauldron. The entire geo was a boiling, foaming white mass, constantly whipped up by the wind and by each 30–40 foot wave smashing into it. Waves breaking into the next geo to the south were sending huge clouds of spray right over the top of the headland, spray which then tore down into and across Whaligoe in twisting white curtains. I made my way down as far as the old harbour buildings, it probably wasn't safe to go any further as the waves were big enough to send water out of the adjacent blowhole, some 50 feet above sea level. I suppose it was nothing particularly out of the ordinary here, but it was certainly the wildest I'd seen.

Back on top I walked a short stretch, at an angle of 45 degrees, along the A9 then headed back across country to Sarclet. The gable end of an old croft provided welcome shelter from the storm for a quick bite to eat; those who only come here on a fine day might wonder why so many of these old cottages are now deserted. A group of four roe deer scampered off, a surprise to see them on the clifftops. They didn't seem bothered by the wind and weather at all, running towards the road but not crossing it and instead heading back north.

Back at Sarclet there remained the problem of getting into the car. Anything such as a rucksack would blow away if put on the ground and the door and boot lid needed to be firmly held or they would probably be ripped off. Suffice it to say that I managed without loss, injury or damage. It was strange indeed to start the engine, turn on the heater and drive off in warmth and comfort with only a slight buffeting from the wind and the swish of the wipers to indicate how wild a day it really was.

Over the Ord

Most of us cross the Ord of Caithness with scarcely a thought, except perhaps in severe weather. Lorry drivers must wish there were a tunnel from Helmsdale to Berriedale. Maybe, some day, millions will be spent on a new route of cuttings, flyovers and tunnels nearer the sea. I hope not. The current route over the Ord is fast enough.

To really appreciate the Ord you should walk it sometime, or at least read the account of Catrine's crossing in Neil Gunn's 'The Silver Darlings'. Much of the old route can still be followed – and once you've done it you'll appreciate how amazing it is to be able to cross the Ord in 15 minutes.

On one of those typical grey November Caithness days I set off from Berriedale to walk over to Navidale and back. A raw, and rising, south-easterly with lowering cloud confirmed the forecast that rain was imminent. A faint path climbs round the hillside above Berriedale harbour, to a prominent stone monument with a seat and a fine view of lorries struggling up the brae to the north. Wild geese flew over, several skeins, disappearing south into the grey murk.

Keeping just above the cliffs, I continued climbing, joining the track which is the old road about half a mile further on. This contours just above steep, broken slopes dropping into the sea and gives a much better impression of the country than the new route. Walking is easy for a mile or so, then the old road curves back inland to join the new route and it's better to carry on by the wall.

Slopes below steepened and it was tempting to keep further inland. Surely that wasn't a ruined croft, in the midst of bracken on steepening downward slopes. It was indeed – one of the outliers of Badbea which, when approached by this route, seems an even more ridiculous spot in which to have expected people to found a settlement. A dreich day is the best to appreciate what life at Badbea was like for the 150 years or so of its habitation. Harsh life or no, some of the residents lived to a ripe old age; the monument records one man who had ten children and died aged 90.

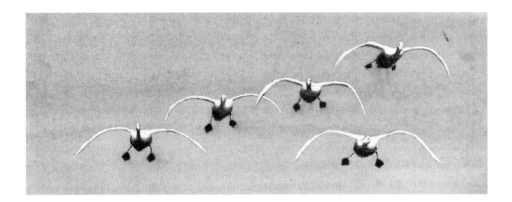

The paths worn out by the villagers still remain, across the stream and along past other scattered houses to the most precariously sited house of all. Here, a double ledge has been cut out from 30-degree slopes leading straight down to the cliff edge, giving room for a house and a small garden patch. Here the children and hens would need to have been tethered, as the stories say they were.

Keeping below the line of the old road, I made my way down into the deep cleft of the Ousdale burn. This is quite an obstacle; you can't get down to the sea as a waterfall bars the way. After days of rain the burn was high, and fast flowing – but there is always a way across. I scrambled up the very steep slopes on the other side, contouring round for a view of the fall, with a seal enjoying the rough breaking seas, then climbed back up onto the gentler slopes of the Ord proper.

From here, a few hundred yards below the modern road, the old route reasserts itself, a choice of two overgrown diagonal rakes descending the hillside to cross the next deep ravine just above the sea. Nobody takes this route any more, there is even a fence across it. The old road then climbs up and down past wartime lookouts before following the cliff edge to Navidale.

Steep, rough slopes climbed up towards the clouds. Suddenly, gliding across the far distant top of the slope in an impossible manner a great white panel appeared, bearing the legend 'SAFEWAY'. Who needs UFOs! (reputedly seen here a few weeks earlier…)

The promised rain was starting now, and I had another crossing of the Ord to make. From Navidale, a tarred road (locked gate) climbs up and up, to a Telecom mast on Creag Thoraidh. Up this road, into the cloud and rain, I tramped, water running down the tarmac in rivers.

On the top, in thick grey mist, the compass was essential for crossing desolate wet bog to the upper Ousdale Burn, then over a ridge to descend out of the mists into the upper Langwell Valley. The best thing about walking by compass is when you eventually emerge more or less where you meant to! A somewhat precarious suspension footbridge took me over the swollen river to the good track which leads back down the Langwell Water to Berriedale. From this valley, and that of the Berriedale Water to the north, the people were evicted a couple of hundred years ago and forced to settle at Badbea.

I always relish a walk down the Langwell valley, particularly as dusk falls on a grey day, and herds of deer move in and out of the birch woods. The woods are dying but at last fencing is taking place to promote regeneration, the fine woods around Langwell show what could be done. It was nearly dark by the time I reached Berriedale, where the two rivers roared under the twin bridges and the damp air smelt of sea and leaf-mould.

I'd seen wild geese, a seal and lots of deer but the best sighting of the day, and I'm not saying where, was of a family of four otters. They didn't see me, and for five minutes I watched them playing in and out of the water, rolling over and over, chasing each other, as at home in the wild November landscape as toddlers by a fireside. You miss a lot when you drive over the Ord in 15 minutes!

The Armadale phone box

Travellers along the North coast would often remark on the Armadale phone box, perched in isolation at the top of a hill overlooking miles of moor and sea. Nowadays it is less isolated, being right next to the new 'motorway' from Strathy to Armadale.

I'd taken a long weekend on the bike, in late November, staying in bothies in the far north-west. Two nights by bothy fires and a day wandering the cliffs, coast and moors... What is it that is so relaxing about hard physical effort in the open air? Or sitting alone by a driftwood fire in a remote bothy on a dark November night? Partly it's that all the complications of modern life are absent. There is nothing to worry about other than the weather and the route. One is free to sit and gaze into the fire and think – without feeling one should be reading a good book, or watching telly, or writing Christmas cards or doing some other job that needs doing.

The second night was windy and wet and I set out at the crack of dawn (actually just as everyone was starting work at Dounreay but time is different in the hills) to cycle down the Lairg road into Tongue. The wind was rising steadily, soon increasingly heavy rain was lashing down in squalls of up to force nine. I was glad it was mostly from behind; the wind howled past on the steep climbs and bowled me along across the tops.

Shelter for lunch was hard to come by and just at the right time I reached the Armadale phone box. It nearly wrenched my arm off to open the door against the wind and as I stood inside buttering and cheesing bread, a particularly vicious squall swept in from the sea. I have not seen such violence of bouncing, sheeting, storm-driven rain for a long time. To open the door would probably have been impossible. I stood, incongruously reading instructions on how to dial Russia or the British Virgin Islands, eating cheese sandwiches and watching the storm lashing the moors with the spray blowing inland over the clifftops from the white sea.

Ralph's Far North

I'm sure I'm not the only one to be thankful for the shelter afforded by that good old solid piece of red Post Office cast iron, even if, in a storm, there was the risk of having to dial 999 to be rescued from it! If the phone box is ever replaced by one of those new all-glass Telecom contraptions it will last just as long as the first real storm.

Oh, how unfit!

My travels have been a bit limited of late, indeed I've not been further afield than Wick or Reay since October. The reason involved a few days enjoying the hospitality of the Caithness General followed by a spell convalescing and getting back to some degree of fitness… Indeed it is a line from Burns' 'Ode to a Haggis' that comes to mind as I'm tempted to get off the bike and walk up Scrabster Brae on a calm morning with not a snowflake or patch of ice in sight 'Oh How Unfit'!

Walking out of hospital is one of life's great experiences, as is the delight of being able to potter a couple of times round the garden. Look out at the familiar view across the county past Dorrery to the Knockfin Heights. Listen to the skeins of wild geese moving off Stemster Loch towards the stubble fields. Then go back into the house for a much-needed rest!

I'm always surprised at how much there is to see and enjoy even if the furthest I can walk is 200 yards along the road. Doing a bit more every day I can fairly soon manage the round walk to the top of Olrig Hill, even if it takes three times longer than usual. That's a place to linger on the sort of calm clear November morning we've enjoyed this year. You appreciate the contrast between the peace of the Great Outdoors and the rush and noise that is so often part of life.

Before dawn, leaning against the trig point, you can watch the streams of headlights converging on Thurso from all directions, and see the ribbon of red tail-lights disappearing over Scrabster Brae towards Dounreay. Yet all is still, the odd grouse cackling, a subdued roar from the breaking waves at Murkle and Dunnet. Seven lighthouses flash. Later on in the day the sound of pile-driving drifts across from Scrabster, six miles away, or if the wind is easterly, the hum from the Norfrost factory. Meanwhile distant skeins of geese come and go, the sun sets red beyond Beinn Ratha and a stream of headlights flows down the Dounreay road into Thurso.

How nice just to amble along Thurso beach and the Victoria walk, watching

the breakers and the wading birds scuttling to and fro. The sea is wonderful anywhere on the North coast even if you haven't the fitness to get far.

No cycling for four weeks I was told. So, four weeks to the day I was off on a gentle ride around Castletown. Once again there is no need to travel long distances or to pedal at great speed to enjoy the countryside. Too many people have been put off cycling because they think it is a strenuous activity. Take it slow and easy, walk the uphill bits and don't think you have to do the time trials or cycle 50 miles. Get a comfortable saddle (a lady's saddle for females) and build up distances gradually, starting with a mile or two. The wooded lanes around Olrig are ideal for a gentle ride.

The ride was about nine miles, my bum was sore and my legs felt like jelly afterwards! But the fresh air, gentle exercise and change of scene did the world of good and soon I was building up the miles again.

I'd not expected to cycle to work much this Winter but the amazing long spell of calm, mild weather tempted me back onto the bike. That really showed how slow I was, but at least the round trip was now possible, without ending up in too much of a heap. The first more roundabout ride home, via Loch Calder, gave a lovely crisp evening, a red sky to the west, geese and swans calling from dark patches on the water, moonlight on a frosted road.

In between days on the bike I had a rest by taking the car, parking in Reay at about seven for a walk or gentle jog up one of the tracks in the early morning gloaming before carrying on to work. It only occurred to me later what rumours might have started as a result of a strange car being seen next to the council houses when people woke up, subsequently driving off before it was properly light!

A walk up into the Reay hills on a fine early morning in December has much to commend it. Initially pitch dark, the sky gradually lightens and the air is laden with moist scents and the sounds of the grouse and wild geese. The burns are heard, not seen, gently rippling over their stony beds. The rush to work seems a long way off. Strangely, few if any citizens of Reay seem to take advantage of the opportunity.

On occasions when I've been fitter I've even managed Beinn Ratha before work, and on lighter mornings have jogged out along the cliffs towards Melvich. If you have to go to work every day why not make the most of the journeys rather than just being another car in the stream of traffic, day in, day out? If I'm not cycling I'll often go down to Crosskirk on the way home for a jog along the cliffs to Brims, or detour to Dorrery for a nip up the hill to see one of the most accessible fine views in the county. At the very minimum I'll walk out past Thurso East or along the beach towards Scrabster.

In Caithness even if you can only walk a few steps or manage the odd mile on the bike there is much to be enjoyed. Potter up the road from Forss towards Bridge of Westfield late on a Winter afternoon, enjoy the damp farmyard smells and the sound of the cows in the byre contentedly munching their silage, watch the sunset and the stars coming out – while almost everyone else hurries past down the main road in a blaze of dazzling headlights intent on getting home as quickly as possible. The higher section of the road gives magnificent views down over the Forss and across to the mountains of Sutherland and you can see some of the hills at the back of Morven which are visible from few other places.

Will I manage Morven before New Year? Perhaps! But if not – well, a gentle walk up Dorrery is still something to look forward to!

The North line

Use it or lose it – all too true about the railways. I fear, however, that unless there is a miracle such as a Dornoch rail crossing, our North line may be doomed whatever we do. So make the most of it while the trains are still running!

People delight in complaining. They forget the vast majority of comfortable, friendly, punctual journeys and dwell on the few occasions when the trains were cold or late. Well, I think the North line is just great. A ride on it is worth any number of soulless Intercity-125 journeys; the staff are friendly and helpful and the new Super Sprinters really are super.

Over the years I've joined or left the train at almost all its stations. What are my immediate memories of the various stops on the line?

Thurso – leaving home at 4.15 AM and walking the five miles to the station to catch the 5.30AM train, clouds of steam from the old steam-heated carriages billowing into the black and frosty early morning.

Wick – walking from Georgemas and catching the train back.

Georgemas – taking friends and relatives to the early train at the crack of dawn; meeting them off the train late at night – standing on the footbridge to watch out for the lights of the approaching train, two miles down the line. An icy January night when the coupling was frozen and the two halves of the train (one for Thurso, one for Wick) needed to be parted by means of buckets of boiling water.

Scotscalder – a real country halt in quiet farmland on the edge of the moors proper. The track to Dorrery through the infamous 'large puddle' where a section is flooded about a foot deep.

Altnabreac – a group of us, dressed in varied cycling and walking garb, taking photos of the train while passengers goggled out of the window at this strangely dressed crowd appearing in the middle of nowhere. Scraping frost from the windows to peer out at the aurora as the train rattles northwards across the moors on an arctic January night.

Forsinard – the old tilley lamp, swaying in the wind on a dark night.

Kinbrace – nine of us alighting before dawn for a 14 hour day of cycling; over Glen Loth, up Strath Brora, up to Ben Armine lodge, wheel the bikes for ten miles over Ben Armine, cycle back to Kinbrace, wave the late train down with the bike lights.

Kildonan – A quiet, grey, January afternoon, pottering by the waterfalls and ruins, watching out for the afternoon train to appear, two miles down the strath. Setting off for a walk to Ben Armine or to Berriedale. Deer.

Helmsdale – a family afternoon outing from Georgemas on a quiet January Saturday afternoon; a walk around the harbour and along the coast, tea in the friendly cafe before catching the train home, with the little boy tucking into 'the best sausages I've ever eaten'.

Brora – getting off the early train with bicycle, a cycle up the strath in early mist and frost, and on by Lairg to Inverness. A round walk over Col Bheinn in summer heat and clouds of flies.

Dunrobin – a family outing by train to see the castle, me feeling utterly ropey whilst under the doctor for an infection, then having to wait over an hour at Golspie for a much delayed train home.

Golspie – collapsing exhausted onto the train with great relief having abandoned an attempt to cycle to Inverness whilst still recovering from a fluey cold. The Big Burn bluebells – look out for them from the viaduct!

Rogart – a station where I've never joined or left the train, but I always think of the sheep sales in progress as the train comes to a halt. And a lost pullover, fallen off the back of the bike somewhere on a nearby hill track.

Lairg – midges on the platform early on an August morning. Brewing tea over a fire in the old waiting room whilst awaiting the late train on a dark December night after a long day on the bike. A grand little woodland walk down to the river, right from the station platform.

Invershin – a dodgy illegal crossing of the bridge on foot to

Culrain – the Carbisdale hostel station; crowds of hostellers getting on and off. Leaving the early train with bikes, cycling up the long Glen Cassley, over hill tracks to Loch Shin and Strath Hope, then a fast 30 mile ride with a following wind to catch the late train home from Kinbrace.

Ardgay – cuckoos calling in May, bluebells by the Firth below the platform. Catching the late train with ten minutes to spare having cycled 20 miles down Glen More and Strathcarron with a flat tyre.

Tain – The guard calling out the station name in pre-Sprinter times on a black night as he walked along the platform. The distillery, looking a lot less romantic from the railway than the glossy adverts suggest. Spending a couple of hours exploring on a late evening while waiting for a replacement train to arrive from Inverness following a breakdown!

Fearn – again, I can hear now the guard shouting out the station name from an unlit platform on a black night in the days before 'on-train announcements'.

Invergordon – always associated with the smelter closure, but a nice place to catch a train north on a crystal clear morning with snow on Wyvis, after taking a shortcut across the Black Isle by bike instead of hanging around in Inverness.

Alness – the start of a grand hill cycling route via Ardross and Strath Rusdale to GlenCalvie and on to Glenbeg.

Dingwall – a place of many associations. Wandering round the town for an hour or two while waiting for the romantic train to Kyle. The friendly Christian bookshop. A four-hour walk in a downpour on the last day of a camping trek to catch the lunchtime train home.

Muir of Ord – in the foothills of the mountains; a station which has several times been the starting point of long treks on foot or by bike. Two 'first days out' come to mind: one walking up the long ridge into the Strathfarrar hills, to camp at nearly 3000 feet; another, in early May, cycling over to Drumnadrochit in drifting snow then on, right through to Glen Shiel and over the Mam Ratagan to arrive at a bothy near Glenelg in the dark.

Inverness is associated with hurried changes of train, of getting on sleepers late at night and off them early in the morning, of leaving bag and a change of clothes in the left luggage lockers and taking off for a run across the Kessock bridge, of delicious cups of tea with bacon and eggs in the station buffet on return.

Our North line is unbeatable for scenery, friendliness and enjoyment of journey. There are few other lines to compare in Britain. Perhaps if we all use it – lots – we won't lose it!

Make the most of life

Those rare brilliantly sunny weekdays at this time of year are frustrating ones on which to be stuck in an office. It's dark when leaving home, dark on getting back and all day long the world outside is sparkling in the low late Autumn sun. Such weather engenders a determination to make the most of the opportunities for a few minutes of freedom during the week even in such seemingly mundane activities as travelling to and from work, or taking a 40-minute lunch break.

Cycling to work at this time of year can be anything from superb to sheer purgatory and all shades in between. The good rides outweigh the bad (I convince myself) and even if much of the ride is in darkness there is still lots to see, and hear, and smell. It's a lot better than going by car or bus, anyway!

What comes to mind about the better aspects of Winter cycling? Pedalling up the long hill from Thurso on a frosty night with the Dunnet lighthouse flashing, Saturn low in the south-west over the dark silhouette of Morven and the countryside already asleep for the long night.

Hammering down the Shebster Brae road past the wood, in shadow from the dawn sun, with the wind from behind. Geese taking off from Loch Calder in the grey dawn. The splashing and quacking of wild ducks. A buzzard soaring over Broubster. Speeding down Scrabster Brae towards the orange lights of Thurso with the bay shimmering under the moon. The Forss waterfall in spate (stop, go down and look!). Empty, moonlit roads, white frost hissing under the bike wheels, a single wheel track miles long. A silent owl dipping and wheeling over the roadside fields.

Then there is lunch-break. Dounreay used to allow a full hour but this was truncated a few years ago to 40 minutes (how many actually take only 40 minutes??) Even in this short time you can still manage quite a bit if you really try. I tear out of site on the bike, bounce up the roads through the old camp and jog up to the top of Cnoc an Freiceadain with its chambered cairn. It's the edge of

another world up here, look there's snow on Ben Hope – and there's the Ola, a dot in the distance heading for Orkney; and see – another skein of wild geese is coming in to join those already feeding on the Achreamie fields. Then hurry back down, pedal back into site barely half an hour after leaving – and there's everybody coming out of the canteen or queuing to buy the lunchtime paper.

Maybe I'll head for Reay, turn down to Isauld Farm, jog down to the sea and along the coast to the sands. Watch the white waves breaking over one of the cleanest beaches in Britain, feel the sun and salt on the face, smell the tangle… Or head back east for a mile, leave the bike and run over the fields to the rockier coast between Dounreay and Forss, scramble down and up onto a little stack overhanging the breaking waves, do a bit of beachcombing in the geo, watch the seals and Eider ducks…

Nobody else ever seems to do these things and even I, to tell the truth, don't always manage to summon up enough determination to climb out of the rut at lunchtime. I suppose the lunatic always considers that everybody else is insane but surely one is meant to strive to make the most of what one's been given in this world!

Highlanders believe in making the day just as long as it has to be. I heartily endorse this, with the proviso that a good night's sleep of at least eight hours is essential so that anything is possible in the remaining 16! It's those odd half-hours, the occasional morning or day, that are so valuable when life is busy and full of responsibilities and much of the week is taken up with work.

A rare morning to spare and I'll be off before seven, rain or dark or gale and back for lunch having climbed Morven or the Griams or run over 15 miles of flow country. There are enough times when one can't for some very good reason, or has a cold – and a morning or afternoon spent lying in bed or watching telly means precious hours of one's life GONE with nothing to show for it.

I'm certainly not saying that everyone should be a physical exercise freak – but please try to do SOMETHING exciting, adventurous, new with those precious minutes of freedom which will never come again. It isn't a cure for the frustration of those brilliantly sunny days glimpsed from an office window, but it certainly helps.

Out to Eribol

It's six o'clock on an austere November Saturday morning. Stars are sharp in a purple sky, there's a faint line of orange in the east and a biting west wind. I pedal cautiously down to Thurso, watching out for ice on the road. As dawn approaches at Shebster the ice crystal streamers from piled shower clouds to the west glow pink and ten minutes later the snow is driving down.

Through Reay it clears, but the Drumholiston road is slushy and I can see the next squall of snow racing in from the west, the moors disappearing into a grey haze. I hurry to cross the Halladale bridge just before it starts; here the road turns north and I can ride up through Melvich in relative shelter as wet snow blows across from the left. It's still only just after eight and nobody is yet abroad.

As the road swings up onto the moor the snow eases off and I can enjoy the ride down the hill to Strathy and warm up again on the steep climb over to Armadale. The wind is slowly getting stronger but on this hilly, twisty road I don't notice it too much. Low sun illuminates the moors and ahead the peaks of Ben Loyal and Hope show white against massed black cloud. A kestrel hovers – it must have good hunting in such sharp, clear air.

Westward, hills steepen, the wind strengthens and it's a steady rhythm of climb up and swing down, hot and cold, sun and squall. A cleansing day of knife-like clarity, nothing soft about it. Either brilliant sun or rattling hailstorm. The colours simple – blue of sky and sea, white wavecrests and snow, orange moor, black and white cloud. The road is empty; today the north coast is mine.

West of Bettyhill I'm at last getting into Sutherland proper. As the wind picks up, progress is slow and I sweat up the steep climb over to Borgie – the hardest on the whole road. There's shelter, briefly by Borgie forest then a very exposed stretch before I reach the lee of the hills above Coldbackie. Past the village I turn sharply down the shortcut to the Kyle, suddenly noticing the scent of larch, and the sea-weed and salt of the estuary. Sun gleams low on esturial sand, oystercatchers call over the causeway, high hills show faintly through thin veils of snow and hail. The wind whips clouds of snow from below the summit of Ben Hope into a great swirling vortex – but it's only practising for the real Winter in a month or two's time.

'Those who feel not the delay nor experience the fatigue nor suffer from the risks and interruptions incident to the former state of the country can but slightly estimate the advantage of its present improved conditions or what it cost to provide them' So reads part of the plaque on the Moin House, built in 1830 for the shelter of travellers. Improved or not, it is hard going today to get there, but the shelter is welcome.

Eribol is flecked white, the gale blowing straight across the loch, but weather systems are moving fast and already there are signs of a change. The last hail roars down at 5PM and as night falls by the loch shore the wind swings gradually round to the south and high cloud veils the stars. By early on Sunday morning steady rain is falling. It's milder, but still cold and wet by the time I get back to the Moin House. The Sutherland peaks are making the weather; to the east it looks brighter and indeed Caithness escapes most of the rain. Briefly at Tongue it clears, there's a gleam of sun and it feels quite muggy but a great black mass is rolling in from the west and the peaks are disappearing one by one.

At Coldbackie the downpour marking the cold front starts. It's the sort of rain that would make you slow to 20MPH in a car. On the bike it's exhilarating racing down through the sheeting water to Borgie and pleasantly cool for the following steep climb. By Bettyhill it's clearing and I strip off and change by the roadside.

Gradually as I head east the sky clears. The sun shines for a couple of hours before sunset, bringing out one or two Sunday afternoon motorists like Winter bluebottles from hibernation. The road home from Thurso is under the stars again with a low quarter moon in the east and a cold wind rising from the south-west, with piled shower clouds silhouetted against the sunset sky.

In November in the Far North, weather IS!

Christmas

Who would get out and about at this time of year. Even I would be tempted to hibernate through December, given the opportunity!

December, particularly in the far North, is dark, dark, dark. Doing normal day work, you might as well be on night shift for all you see of the daylight. People are busy, tired and cross. There is far too much to do. Cycling to work becomes a daily struggle; only driving daily in the traffic and ice and dark would be worse!

The modern ways of 'celebrating' Christmas and New Year have a lot to answer for. Feasting is fine when you don't have enough to eat for most of the year. Spending a day or two indoors by the fireside with the family is great if the rest of the year is spent fighting the hostile elements on the land.

Why should the celebration of love, peace and joy take weeks of preparation, getting everyone tired and irritable in the process? Do you really enjoy days of overeating and drinking, putting on weight, watching the telly and videos for hours, perhaps even days? Or do you just do it because everyone else and all the adverts say you should? Christmas and New Year seem to have merged into one long celebration of materialism.

Just for a minute, think of what we are really celebrating at this time of year. For Christians it is the birth of a child, in the simplest, messiest circumstances. For all it marks the turning of the year, when the days start to lengthen. The New Year is a time to think of fresh starts, new beginnings.

How do you really want to mark these things? Is it through exhausting yourself and losing your temper in lots of preparation, putting yourself in debt and then spending more days in lethargy and over-indulgence?

The hill-gangrels who go off to the bothies at New Year have in my opinion got it more nearly right. The simpler and more real the occasion, the more you can celebrate what this time of year is all about. What could be better than a group of friends seeing in the New Year round a bothy bog-wood fire, miles from the nearest television or even electricity – and then first-footing the hills the next day, in blizzards, driving rain or even sunshine!

Christmas at Cape Wrath! The owners of a bothy, situated a couple of miles from the lighthouse, have the right idea; the bothy book records a number of such expeditions they made from the far south. Feasting and laziness when we already have plenty to eat and too little exercise will always turn out to be a hollow celebration. How much better a Christmas dinner cooked over a fire after an epic struggle to reach the bothy!

Certainly my most memorable days at the turn of the year have been the simplest, days spent out on the moors and mountains, days of gales and sleet and driving rain, days of hard frost and snow. The best Christmas lunch is a box of sandwiches when you're ravenous after stumbling and crawling through gales since before dawn. The best New Year drink is a cup of hot sweet tea from a vacuum flask, crouched in the lee of some frost-hoary cairn as the grey late-afternoon mist swirls past.

The farmer who's been out bielding his sheep from the storm and foddering his cattle is the man who comes in and really deserves his Christmas roast. Most of us would do better fasting instead. The council workman who's been gritting and ploughing roads round the clock is the man who really deserves his New Year dram.

Many people who cannot have close family around them feel lonely and left out. Once again the emphasis is wrong; this is not a time of year to look inwards to the family circle but to to look outwards. I greatly admire those who spend Christmas and New Year helping the people sleeping on our city streets and only regret I haven't the guts to do likewise. Isn't it an indictment of our selfish society that the suicide rate is highest at this time of year!

I don't mean to be a kill-joy. But Christmas and New Year should be about real joy. Expensive presents, drunken parties, television films give only a poor substitute. The story tells that the joy came to shepherds out in the snow, to a smelly byre among the animals, not to Herod in his palace. Celebrate simply. Get out, feel the wind and hail and sleet, remember the real world and say no to the poor materialistic substitute so many in the West try to make do with!

A flake or two of snow

In the good old days you'd be cut off by a blizzard until the snow melted. Nowadays you have to try and get to work, or school, come what may...

Living on a hill in the north of Scotland guarantees interesting Winter conditions. After a night of drifting snow it was no surprise to see two-foot drifts across the gate and foot-deep drifts along the road. In such conditions a bike is ideal, to pedal the easy stretches between the drifts and wheel it through the deep snow. The snow was soft, powdery and dry, and for the only morning of the week the ride into Thurso was quite pleasant. The bike hissed softly through the snow in the dark, only getting stuck in the odd deeper drift. There was a strong wind from the side though, with still some spindrift.

Heavy, driving snow came on as I reached town just after seven and, combined with the gale and pitch darkness, it was too dangerous to carry on in traffic. The bus took me the rest of the way to work that morning. As dawn broke at Dounreay the scene was as wild as I've ever seen it there. All was white – land, air and sea. Thirty-foot breakers were smashing up the shore on a high tide, sending spray at least twice as high into the air. Even right on the coast, the gale was drifting fine snow. I was looking forward to a good run round the site inspecting the coast at lunchtime but we were sent home early. A nice opportunity for some cross-country skiing in the afternoon, after digging the gate clear.

The wind rose, the snow fell. I needn't have bothered clearing the gate; after a night of gales and snow it was completely buried under a drift seven feet deep. The road, where it ran between stone walls, had simply filled up. Not even a tractor could get along and needless to say, for the second day running, the school bus didn't make it either. There was no way I was going to get to work!

The day was instead mostly spent out of doors, moving the several tons of snow which now blocked the gate and taking a break from time to time to do a bit of skiing. In such really deep drifts skis are the ideal way of getting about.

Around lunchtime a snowplough appeared along the road, but took nearly an hour to reach our house. The crew gave up at that point, the road onwards was even worse, a digger would be needed.

On the next morning I set out down the supposedly cleared road, earlier than usual at 6.15. A brief thaw the previous evening and a little rain had now frozen, leaving the snow-covered road in a dreadful state. Somehow I managed about three miles on the rutted, icy surface, periodically finding myself sliding along the road ahead of the bike. I had to walk the last mile downhill, and even this was difficult on the ice. Once in town conditions improved though a little slush on the Dounreay road still made the cycling a bit dodgy.

Back at home, at first light, a snowplough appeared from the other direction with, behind it, the school bus! Unfortunately the plough was on the other side of a long stretch of deep drifts and took so long to get through that the bus gave up and was seen disappearing, in reverse, into the distance. Another day off school… Meanwhile a big digger arrived and managed to partly demolish the garden dry-stane dyke while attacking the drift on the corner. The bike-ride home from Thurso that night was like a ski-slalom through ruts and slush and bumpy ice in the dark, the road a canyon between five-foot drifts.

That night it snowed and blew again; Thurso residents noticed a little fresh snow but at home all the snow from miles of fields had collected into fresh two-foot drifts along the road. I dragged and wheeled the bike for half a mile through the worst and then managed to cycle the rest, after a fashion, all over the road, slipping, sliding, bumping. The bike was getting a dreadful pounding but fortunately was already only fit for the scrapheap. The wind was rising and I'd had enough by the time I'd reached town. There was just time to catch the bus again.

Buses are wonderful and my favourite form of transport (after a bike). Just to sit back, let the driver do all the worrying about the road conditions, to be carried effortlessly along through the black stormy morning and get to work well on time!

Back at home, the school bus was making a brave attempt on the road which hadn't yet been ploughed. Having managed to reach our house it then, to the delight of the children on board, set off to run the remaining drifts. To their even greater delight it managed about 200 yards and got thoroughly stuck. Next, the snowplough arrived from the other direction to find the road blocked by the bus. After an hour of digging, pulling and ploughing all were eventually extricated but the condition of the road was such that the bus driver was instructed to take the children back home. Another day off school!

Come Friday and the road had been thoroughly ploughed, salted and gritted. The school bus came on time and got to school on time. Unfortunately the school heating had failed and all the children were sent back home.

By nightfall it was snowing hard again as I pedalled homewards … Far better in the old days when you just stayed at home.

Three Winter days

Three Winter days, all different, and yet alike…

A mid-December day, one of the darkest of the year. Calm and foggy, rare weather indeed for the Far North. An occasional spit of drizzle or the lightest puff of wind were the only things to change, though occasionally the cloud would lift to give a misty couple of miles visibility below a grey sheet at 200 feet. This was a day for the coast, a good day for cycling without having to fight winds.

Castletown was still dark, the Dunnet road was empty in the grey early light, Scarfskerry was just waking. Further on, leaving the bike, I crossed a misty headland and clambered down to a bay where 20 or 30 seals splashed from rocks out into the sea. Their heads bobbed near the water's edge, watching this lone intruder walk their empty shore.

Mist came and went on the coast road but had lifted enough for Stroma to be visible from John O'Groats. Although it was late morning almost nobody was about and the harbour was deserted other than for a pair of eider duck. The top of the Duncansby stacks rose into the fog, while below, the quiet grey rocky beaches gave a peace that in Summer is never found even at this relatively remote spot.

Back along the coast at Brough the tide was out, permitting a slippery crossing over seaweedy rocks to the stack. A bevy of seals splashed and snorted into the water leaving one, marooned in the middle of the exposed rocks, which snarled and hissed at me from a few yards away.

There was still time for a detour out to Dunnet Head, to watch the lighthouse beam sweeping out into the fog as dusk turned to dark on one of the shortest days of the year.

Christmas Eve by contrast was a day of sharp, cold clarity. A strong south-west wind, clear skies, hills 50 miles away crisp-white on the horizon but the nearer landscape still awaiting the first real snowfall. Beyond the horizon rose

great wispy cumulonimbus, giving storms and blizzards on the west coast. The low sunlight was almost harsh, casting long shadows. Lochs were dark blue amid yellow-brown moors and the bog pools had a thin crust of ice.

The bitter headwind gave hard cycling in the dark before dawn out to Westerdale and on to Loch More, but was more from the side for the run to Altnabreac, with the sun now up. Soft sand can make cycling these roads almost impossible, but on this occasion everything was frozen hard and only a few ruts required care. I carried on west, almost as far as Strath Halladale before leaving the roads and striking north across the heart of the flow country. An obvious route, linking a string of five remote lochs, leads to the end of the Shurrery Lodge track. To drag and wheel the bike this way was hard work, but worth the effort to traverse the heart of Caithness in the depths of Winter.

By what is, arguably, the remotest loch in the county, a strange thing happened. A bird looking like a grouse appeared, flying straight towards me and the bike. It landed about four feet away; it was dumpy, much smaller than a grouse and a very handsome speckled brown. As I watched in amazement it sat for a few seconds then scuttled a few feet and disappeared into a peaty hole at the water's edge. I could see it there, sitting motionless below a little peat overhang and could have reached down and stroked it. The only bird that fitted, from the books, was a quail – but such had no right to be in the middle of the flows in December.

I wandered up onto Ben Nam Bad Mor, one of my favourite local hills, to see the sunset over the moors. A couple of arctic hares seemed almost tame, only running off in a very unconcerned manner when just a few yards away. A thin layer of snow covered the summit; more would soon be coming!

A week later – Hogmanay, lying snow, frost, and brilliant sunshine belying a dreadful forecast. In some trepidation I drove the icy road down Strath Halladale in the early morning; there had been some drifting near Forsinard but the road was passable and I carried on over the bealach to leave the car a couple of miles on by the old roadside cottage.

I'm always wary about leaving the car for hours on such a day as a rising wind and drifting snow can quickly block roads but the weather looked set fair, with showers staying well to the west.

Cross-country skis gave steady progress over the deep snow-covered heather, with frozen dubh-lochs giving particularly easy going. After an hour I was climbing up towards the plateau, cutting across the slopes at an easy angle. Behind, the pure white slopes of the Griams, Ben Armine and the Sutherland hills looked incredibly remote – then came a familiar sound, and there was the two-coach Sprinter heading northwards looking like a toy train in wonderland. It must have been a superb ride from Inverness on such a day!

The sun appeared over the skyline, and soon I was on the ridge, heading south for the highest part of the Knockfin Heights. The skiing was quite slow, with grasses and heather showing through the snow, but vastly easier than slogging knee-deep on foot.

Views on such a day from the hills are beyond my humble powers of description. Actually, most of a white Caithness was visible, with the sea and Hoy in the distance, the Morven-Scaraben range, as well as all the Sutherland hills from Golspie to Klibreck,and from Ben Hee to Ben Hope. The wind was cold, but not that cold, and moderated as the day wore on.

For an hour I skied around the Knockfin plateau, the frozen lochans giving excellent going. This is a place to visit either on a day such as this, or in June when the birdlife is at its best. Or go on a misty day in November for a test of route-finding – but don't forget the compass!!

I managed to find gentle slopes down which even I could ski with only a couple of falls, and with surprisingly little effort was back at the car as the sun was setting. In the last hour of daylight of the year I carried on down to the shores of Loch an Ruathair, the track giving some of the best skiing of the day.

A full moon was rising above Meall a Bhealaich and the frost was setting in harder as the silent white hills awaited the New Year.